TAROT READING MADE EASY

The Newbies Guide to Psychic Tarot Reading, Simple Tarot Spreads, Understanding Tarot Cards and Their Meanings, Become More Intuitive, and Discover Your True Purpose!

By
Shelly O'Bryan

© Copyright 2019 by Shelly O'Bryan - All rights reserved.

This book is provided with the sole purpose of providing relevant information on a specific topic for which every reasonable effort has been made to ensure that it is both accurate and reasonable. Nevertheless, by purchasing this book you consent to the fact that the author, as well as the publisher, are in no way experts on the topics contained herein, regardless of any claims as such that may be made within. As such, any suggestions or recommendations that are made within are done so purely for entertainment value. It is recommended that you always consult a professional prior to undertaking any of the advice or techniques discussed within.

This is a legally binding declaration that is considered both valid and fair by both the Committee of Publishers Association and the American Bar Association and should be considered as legally binding within the United States.

The reproduction, transmission, and duplication of any of the content found herein, including any specific or extended information will be done as an illegal act regardless of the end form the information ultimately takes. This includes copied versions of the work physical, digital and audio unless express consent of the Publisher is provided beforehand. Any additional rights reserved.

Furthermore, the information that can be found within the pages described forthwith shall be considered both accurate and truthful when it comes to the recounting of facts. As such, any use, correct or incorrect, of the provided information will render the Publisher free of responsibility as to the actions taken outside of their direct purview. Regardless, there are zero scenarios where the original author or the Publisher can be deemed liable in any fashion for any damages or hardships that may result from any of the information discussed herein.

Additionally, the information in the following pages is intended only for informational purposes and should thus be thought of as universal. As befitting its nature, it is presented without assurance regarding its prolonged validity or interim quality. Trademarks that are mentioned are done without written consent and can in no way be considered an endorsement from the trademark holder.

TABLE OF CONTENTS

Introduction 1

Chapter 1 *Introducing The Tarot* 3

Chapter 2 *The Major Arcana* 11

Chapter 3 *The Minor Arcana* 24

Chapter 4 *Imagery Symbolism In The Cards* 32

Chapter 5 *Detailed Card Descriptions: Major Arcana* 41

Chapter 6 *Exploring Spreads* 56

Chapter 7 *Interpreting Your Spread* 63

Chapter 8 *Practice Examples* 69

Chapter 9 *Intuition Development For Insightful Readings* 79

Chapter 10 *Reading For Others* 82

Conclusion 85

Description 87

INTRODUCTION

Congratulations on purchasing *Tarot Reading Made Easy* and thank you for doing so.

Within the most recent years, the curiosity in tarot and tarot reading has developed exponentially. The tarot is a collection of 78 different cards with pictures that have been known to be used for centuries to make known concealed facts. More and more people are trying to live their lives more creatively and they are looking for ways to intermingle their outer and inner realities. Many have discovered that tarot is a powerful tool for growth and discovery. The main purpose of this book is to inform you about what tarot actually is and to teach yourself how to use the cards. Using the cards will help you appreciate yourself on a deeper level and you'll learn how to tap into your inner being more confidently. Contrary to popular belief, to successfully read the tarot, you do not have to have "psychic powers". The only things you will need are belief and willingness to develop your natural intuitive abilities.

Tarot Reading Made Easy will be broken down into multiple chapters. The following chapters will discuss in detail what tarot is, history, myths and facts about tarot, how to get started with your own readings, what major and minor arcana are and the differences between the two, the meanings of each card, the different types of spreads based on the reading, exercises to practice card pulling, how to do readings for yourself and for others, the cards and their descriptions, image symbolism, and how to develop intuitive insight for your readings. Once you have completed this book, you should be well on your way to doing your first successful tarot pulls and readings.

If it is possible for you as a student to work with a qualified tarot instructor, we strongly advise you to do so in correlation with reading this book on tarot. Learning tarot is usually very fun and interactive in a small group setting, and there really is no substitute for in-person lessons. We also encourage you to become a member of free tarot groups to immerse yourself into the practice and lean on others who are learning tarot and those that are highly qualified in tarot pulling and readings. Feel free to look back on this book as you progress through your tarot practices. It is a great reference tool in the event you forget some information, or you come across a situation that is completely new to you and you are not sure how to proceed.

Each card reading and meaning will always be subjective to the person who is pulling the card. There is never a set meaning for one card that applies exactly the same way each time you see the card in your pulls. This is why tarot spreads are becoming increasingly popular. The spread assigns a set meaning to various card positions, allowing the card pulled to that position to reflect that meaning. A true understanding of tarot and how the cards affect one another heightens the understanding of each spread. This understanding comes from hands-on experience with the tarot cards.

There are plenty of books on beginning a journey to tarot reading on the marketplace, so we appreciate you for your choice in this one! Every attempt was made to make sure it is filled with as much useful information as possible. Please take pleasure in your reading!

CHAPTER 1
Introducing The Tarot

The starting point of the tarot is truly a work of anonymity. We are aware that tarot cards were first discovered in Europe in the late 14th century. They were used in Italy as a popular card game. The tarot has four suits like most common card games. Varying by region, the suits are different. French suits come from North Europe, Latin suits in South Europe, and there were German suits in Central Europe. Every suit contains 14 cards, ten cards of which were numbered from one (Ace) to ten known as pip, and four cards with faces (King, Queen, Knight, and Jack/Knave). In addition, the tarot has a single card that is referred to as the Fool, which is separated from the original suit as well as a 21-card trump suit. These newest decks were referred to as *carte da trionfi*, or trump cards and supplementary cards are known as *trionfi*, which turned into "trumps" in the English language. The original documentation of the word trionfi was found in a printed court account of records in Florence in 1440. In Florence, the expanded deck of 97 cards was called *Minchiate*. The cards include the four elements and astrological symbols, as well as the tarot motifs that were traditional. Sigismondo Pandolfo Malatesta regarded the movement of two decks. These tarot cards are still used to play common card games throughout much of Europe but without the occult symbology. The wealth of this century was known to commission beautiful decks of their own, and some have survived the times. One of the earliest and most complete decks was created around 1450. It became known as the Visconti-Sforza.

The tarot is a collection of visual symbols that were designed to relate meaning and mystery specifically to a variety of symbols. The images illustrate a life that was long past human evolution. The images are a reflection of timeless human values in what can be considered primitive structures of politics. Even with this, it was considered a study guide that was highly useful for seeking personal advancement and predicting future events. More often than not, people use tarot to predict their futures. Whether it can be about a job promotion or a lover, people are usually generally interested in using tarot to find out about future events. Ultimately, the tarot is widely misunderstood by the general public because of the mystery of it. The relationship it has with the occult gives tarot a bad name, and most people shy away from tarot readers for this reason. Those who are super religious believe that tarot is the work of evil, or that it brings life to things that we as humans have no business knowing.

The mystery and spookiness of the tarot only last until you make the commitment to learn it and use it effectively. The study of tarot is not something that can be perfected overnight. With the most widely used practices, there is a variety of levels of understanding the tarot. Many people spend years learning the tarot and finding out what spreads work best for them personally, and the people that they offer readings to. These range from simple readings to working with the cards and advanced magical techniques to affect your life in a positive way. Even some of the best tarot readers in the world typically only use the practice to shed light on a question that is being asked, either for current use or for knowledge of the future. Although tarot can be used with magic to effect change, it's not always recommended to use the practice this way. It is important to respect the craft and study it well enough to understand all the different aspects of it. The tarot as a system has evolved over the centuries. Many artists have put their own touches on custom decks of cards that are available for purchase all over the world. These illustrations typically enchase the preferred meanings of the cards themselves. They also are known to eliminate others. These cards have expanded over the last few decades to include different perspectives from cultures around the world. There are now Japanese, herbal, mythological, and Native American inspired decks. The origin cards, however, remain relatively the same. Although the meanings of the cards have been altered or changed completely, the mystery behind the cards still remains. People will continuously argue on the origins of the tarot and what exactly the symbolism stands for or their hidden meanings. The tarot has changed over time, but the effectiveness of the practice has not changed.

A traditional tarot reading usually involves a seeker and a reader. A seeker is the person who is asking the question to be answered by the card pull and spread. It is common to only ask one question to be answered per spread. Most questions are personal, either relating to how a person feels or something they want to know about their future. It is extremely important for the seeker to keep their questions as simple as possible. Especially with being new to tarot, it is important to not overwhelm yourself with the complexity of it. One thing that would be extremely useful for a new seeker would be to have a list of tarot keywords readily available when pulling a spread. Using a keyword chart will definitely help you in your reading. When beginning your tarot journey, forget the detailed meanings for now. It will be important to study long-term, but in the beginning, it is not necessary to know. If you want to get started with readings quickly, keywords are the best starting point. Use keywords that trigger your personal connection to the cards and what you want to expect with the cards in your readings. It is typical to find that just one word that has a personal connection will bring up many different concepts and deeper meanings that will help with your reading.

The reader in the tarot reading is the person who has practiced how to understand the cards. Once the seeker has mixed up the cards to their liking, they will cut the deck in half. This action is so that the cards are in place based on the seeker and their needs rather than the reader shuffling the deck for them. It is important that the cards are based within the spirit of the seeker in order to get a fulfilling reading based on the question the seeker is looking for an answer for. Once the seeker has completed these actions, the reader will then pull and lay out the cards based on the spread they are performing. Different spreads can be used for different questions or the answers the seeker is looking to obtain. Every single place in the spread has significance, and every individual card in that position has a connotation as well. The job of the person who reads is to combine the meaning of both the position and the card to bring a better understanding to the seeker on their question. Additional cards may be pulled depending on how the spread is pulled. Sometimes, the combination of the position and the card does not give a very clear reading and therefore the reader can pull a clarity card to help read a better understanding to the answer that was given for the question asked by the seeker.

The process of pulling a tarot spread really is simple, but everything that is shown to people through movies and TV makes people believe that it is anything but simple. It is most common for people to see a tarot spread being pulled in a dark room with crystal balls in a creepy parlor, whether it is in TV shows or in the movies. The reader is typically an older lady wrapped in beautiful scarves with a faint accent. She is seated in the darkest part of the room, barely showing her face to those who enter the room. The seeker tends to be a young girl, desperate to know the answer to a question usually pertaining to her future or her love life. The girl will ask the question and the reader will begin pulling her cards for her. The suspense will build as the cards are pulled until the reader pauses for a moment before pulling the final card. The ominous woman pulls the final card, setting it down in the center of the spread. She looks up at the young girl as she places her finger on the death card. The young girl looks at the card in horror, frightened over her impending misfortune.

Even in today's time, there is an aura of darkness that clings to the tarot. There are quite a few religions that shun the tarot and its practices and promotes them as elements of evil. Scientific establishments also condemn them as symbols of unreason or elements of a past that has not yet to be enlightened. It is important for people to take the creepy element out of the history of tarot to see it for what it really is. The tarot is simply a deck of elaborately decorated picture cards. It is hard for us as a society to take the emotional element out of something that has long been considered a controversy to see it for what it really is. To really understand the tarot, it is important to go beyond what it is. You must dig deeper inside of not only the deck of cards but also within yourself. Whether you want to be a seeker or a reader or both, this is the first step in truly starting your tarot journey. Once this is realized and practiced, we can begin to answer the question that arrives shortly after. What can we do with these cards?

As you will begin to realize through your tarot journey, the answers lie within the subconscious mind. The subconscious is one of the deepest levels of not only memory but also the awareness that lies within each and every one of us from the moment we are born. The subconscious is always a part of us, although it happens and functions outside of our everyday living. More often than not, we tend to ignore the functions of the subconscious as it is not something we need to get through our daily lives. Yet, it has been known to affect each and every decision we make day in and day out. The subconscious was even talked about in the writings of Sigmund Freud. He believed and thought that it was the habitat of our deepest intolerable urges and needs. Carl Jung however wrote about the constructive aspects of the subconscious. He saw the positive and creative aspects of the subconscious. He wrote to express the collective aspect of it that was able to touch widespread traits. It is likely we will never know the true power and depth of the subconscious, but studying the tarot helps us navigate the landscape. There are other things that have been developed to explore the subconscious that is typically used in conjunction with the tarot. These include psychotherapy, dream interpretation, meditation, and visualization. If you already are someone who studies one of these aspects on the subconscious, think about the way that you can also bring the tarot into this. You will see that the tarot can be a successful guiding light into understanding the deeper levels of your mind and memory. There are so many positive aspects of practicing tarot, and getting to know you better on a deeper level is only one of them. Many people use therapy to understand themselves and why they do the things they do. You could consider the tarot as a form of therapy. Imagine the possibilities of understanding and eventually healing you can do for yourself and for others if you do decide to start reading tarot for others.

Tarot power comes from a collective of universal and personal understanding. Each individual card can have its own meaning to you personally, but the cards are also supported by a universal understanding of what the card means. As in, how the world collectively views the cards. It is wise to remember that each card reflects back onto you your own individual uniqueness and the hidden aspects of your own awareness. Although there are elements of a tarot pulling and spread we believe to be at random, the shuffling, cutting, and dealing of the cards, tarot readers and seekers still truly believe that we chose those cards at the pulling for a reason. You can shuffle a deck as many times as you want, but the cards that need to appear to you for the specific spread you are doing will always appear to you on the top of the deck. The whole reasoning of a tarot spread is to pull the cards we were destined to observe. General sense informs us that the cards are shuffled and pulled as random, but digging deeper can reveal the true sense of what cards were pulled and why.

When practicing tarot, it can feel as though the results of the pull are coming to us by chance. We know that in each shuffling and pulling of the deck, we are actively involved in every step. It is not as though the cards are shuffled on their own and are magically pulled from the top of the deck and laid in a spread that we are not initially choosing to use. Each of us has an inner guide that is used during tarot to act as a vehicle to awareness. This inner guide is what draws us to a certain number of shuffles and cuts that create our deck for our spread. You cannot destroy this connection to your inner self, but you can choose to ignore it if you want to. However, when you reach for a tarot deck, you are having a conversation with your inner self about being open to its wisdom and to lead us into the direction that we need to go. You allow yourself to be completely in control of the situation until you open up and allow your inner guide to take the reins. It is in our nature to rely on our inner guide and somewhere along the way of human development we forgot how to regularly access it. We tend to rely on our conscious mind a great deal, and forget to tap into the unconscious. Although the conscious mind is known to be much clearer, it does not necessarily have all the means we need to have full awareness to make appropriate choices every single day. Life seems to have more purpose when we operate fully out of our conscious mind and it may feel as though situations happen to us by chance encounters. Ultimately, as humans, we tend to suffer because we do not know what we truly want and quite honestly who we are. Think about that for a minute. Within our conscious mind, we do not know who we are and what we want from life. It is with accessing our subconscious mind that we can begin to explore these areas. Only once we have explored our subconscious can we begin to experience life differently. There is ultimately a level of peace experienced once our inner self and conscious are aligned with one another. We become more fulfilled by our choices and see that life experiences are a way of interacting with our subconscious and inner self by making decisions to steer our own path in the way that we are meant to go.

Think of the tarot as the easiest way to access your inner self and become more aware within your subconscious. It is one of the best tools to help guide you to a new way of thinking outside of your daily life and conscious mind. You will see that the cards pulled and the images that emerge from the reading are a sign from your inner self and what it wants you to know. More often than not, feelings emerge from a reading, and this is also a way for your inner self to speak to you through tarot. Obviously, it is hard to know within your conscious mind that there really is a message coming from the cards, but it is up to you to tap into your inner self to understand that there is a message and how to interpret it based on the question you asked your inner self to reveal an answer to.

Now that you have a better understanding of what the tarot is, where it came from and what it can do for you, it is time to begin your journey through reading the tarot. The following chapters will dig deeper into the different aspects of the tarot and how to use these aspects towards your future practices. Know that you can refer back to this book at any moment in your journey for clarification or to remember something you may have forgotten. Each journey to tarot is different for every one of us, but it is good to have the support and solid ground to get started. Trust your experiences and see what happens! If you are ultimately focused on gaining access to your inner self, you do not necessarily need the tarot to achieve this. The tarot cards can be a guide to your inner self until you have reached your optimal potential to access and understand your subconscious and inner self on your own without guidance. At this point, you can consider whether or not it is your choice to bring the tarot into others' lives to help them do the same. Ultimately, your tarot journey is up to your discretion. You can take it as far as you want to, knowing that you are supported every step of the way. This book in conjunction with the tarot and its practice will help you reach whatever goals you set for yourself as a reader and seeker of the tarot. We are excited to see where this journey takes you!

CHAPTER 2
The Major Arcana

The traditional tarot deck of cards is made up of 78 cards. These cards are broken into two sections. These sections are referred to as the major arcana and the minor arcana. In this section, we will be discussing the major arcana in detail so you can get a better understanding of these cards, what they are meant for, and what you can do with them in your tarot journey. The major arcana are the symbolic picture cards in a traditional tarot deck. There are typically around 22 of these types of trump cards in a standard tarot deck. Before the 17th century, these trump cards had little to no magical importance. They were just simply a part of a special deck that was used for gaming and gambling. Arcana is the plural version of the word *Arcanum*. Arcanum has a simple definition meaning a profound secret. Those of the Middle Ages, including alchemists, considered the Arcanum to be the secrets of the natural world. This is why the tarot as a whole is commonly referred to as a collection of secrets. These cards are said to enlighten our world.

These 22 cards that make up the major arcana in the full tarot are considered the heart of the deck. It is known that each card is a representation of some universal aspects of the human experience. This relates to all of the different experiences we face as humans throughout our lifetime. Each major Arcanum represents a scene, usually consisting of one person or multiple people, with many symbolic events taking place within each card. In most decks, these major arcana cards also consist of a number, usually written in Roman numerals. Some may also have a unique name per each card, while others may only have the picture depicted. The earliest recorded decks were free from numbers and names on the majors, as it is likely that many of the people that used them did not know how to read and write. There are many cards whose names represent their meanings directly. These cards include Strength, Justice, and Temperance. These typically are depicted by individuals who represent that specific meaning. The additional cards are persons who represent a meticulous approach to a living situation. Examples of these cards include the Hermit and the

Magician. There are also cards that refer to astrological elements. These include the Star, the Moon, and the Sun. These cards are said to represent the forces associated with heavenly bodies, most commonly elusive to the human state.

The major arcana cards have long been considered special because of the complex reactions they draw out of seekers and readers alike. The images on a specific set of tarot cards, the Universal-Waite set, are suggestive because they unite the imagery of the tarot with people and situations that are recognizable to everyday human life. The symbolism is simple but effective. It is easy for a seeker to relate the images they see on the cards to different situations they have experienced in their own lives. It is important to make this connection because this is how you will understand what the card symbolizes in your spread based on the question that you want to be answered. Having a major arcana card pulled during a spread is important because there is a heavier weight placed on its position within the spread. It will mean more to the seeker in its specific pull position than if a different card was pulled to be in that position.

A major card is always given more power when it is pulled in a reading. It typically means that when a major arcana card is pulled, the issues that are at stake in the spread will not be short-lived or temporary. Major arcana cards represent the most basic concerns felt by humans. They also stand for your most major feelings and the motivations that push you through your life. In other words, these cards are the depiction of humanity's spiritual evolution into the enlightenment era and becoming individualized. When many of these cards show up in a single pull, it expresses that now is the time of high importance for the seeker. The seeker should think through each card that is pulled because it is important they act upon the spread in a way that would positively benefit them and the question that is being answered within the spread. Depending on what card is pulled, the seeker can act upon the question based on the personal or universal meaning of the card.

The major arcana are often considered a collective unit or the 22 cards being one whole unit. Many artists have illustrated the cards to have different schemes to show how the cards shape patterns.

These patterns shed radiance on the human state. There are three different things that often play a role in these schemes. These things are numerology, astrology, and other esoteric sciences. These cards are known to show the journey of a person from birth to enlightenment. These cards are often seen as the illustrated depiction of an individual's voyage through inner expansion. The expedition is often referred to in the tarot world as the Fool's Journey. In this journey, the cards are standing for an experience or personal quality that we must incorporate into our own lives, to realize our wholeness or have a deep understanding of our inner self. This travel down the road to self-actualization is something many people find to be a lifelong journey. Self-actualization is referred to as the realization or fulfillment of one's talents and potentialities, most often considered as a drive or a need to present in everyone. Tarot is a useful tool for people who are on this journey to getting to know their inner self. It is a guiding light in an experience that can leave many unsure of even where to begin. A strong desire to know you on a deeper level is important when reaching a level of self-actualization. These trips down the road to self-actualization often involve diversions. There are step backs and start overs more often than a smooth succession through the process. Everyone has a specific path that is unique to them as a person. It is normal to screw up and make mistakes, but it all is a part of the lesson in realizing our own potential. It is common to lack courage. This courage is needed to evoke insight to find out our deep down levels. The Hermit card is the call to look to our innermost self, and some people will never hear the call. Those who do not hear the call may never experience a catastrophe of the Tower. This disaster of the Tower might liberate them from ego resistance, but they are never given the opportunity to experience this.

This is an opportunity to expand on the journey that is referred to as the Fool's Journey. It is one of the most commonly talked about aspects of the tarot when you are learning it for the first time. The journey is a symbol for an individual's journey from beginning to end their own unique existence. Of the 22 cards that make up the major arcana, each card is a representation of each stage of the journey. This is an experience within life a person must integrate in order to understand completeness. The 22 different images are made on certain keywords that are representative of each major arcana card. For ease of reading, the keywords for each card will be bolded and the numeric representation of the card will be represented in parenthesis. We will get into the deeper descriptions and meaning of each card in later chapters, but this will give you an overview as to what to expect from each card once we get to that section.

The journey begins with the Fool card (0), a card that represents **beginnings**. The Fool is each and every one of us, as we begin our journey through life. This can be imagined as a person at birth. This person is a fool simply because they are a new soul with innocent **faith** in themselves to undertake a journey that is likely to cause pain and require them to experience hazards and wrong turns. At the beginning of the trip to self-awareness, the fool is an infant who is fresh, **spontaneous**, and open to new experiences. The illustration on the card is of a person with their arms wide open, from side to side, and their head held high with sights toward the sky. The person on the card is open to embrace whatever happens to come their way. It should be noted that the person on the card is also very oblivious to the fact that the edge of the cliff is near. It appears as though he is about to move across, regardless of the cliff ending. The Fool is not aware of the difficulties they will be faced with as they venture out on their own to experience the world for themselves. This is where they begin to learn the lessons the world has to offer them. The Fool is somewhat on the outside of the remainder of the major arcana. Zero is often not considered in a numerical sequence. On a number line, it lies right in the middle of the number system, equal distance from both negative and positive. At conception, the Fool is set in the center of its own world. The Fool starts out somewhat empty but has the desire to go forth and learn. The undertaking of these adventures for the Fool seems like **stupidity**. But is it really?

Once the Fool has set out on the adventure, they will immediately run into the High Priestess (2) and the Magician (1). These two cards are the harmonizing forces that make up the world the way it is perceived. In the material universe, these cards are a representation of a feature that says as rapidly as we name a feature of an incident, we immediately also create the opposite of the experience. The Magician is known as the optimistic side of the experience. He represents the **active**, male power of a creative desire. It can also be considered our **conscious awareness** of a situation. The Magician is a guide that allows us to contact our earth through a **concentration** of personality, **power,** and will. Alternatively, the High Priestess is the pessimistic side of the circumstances. She is the **unexplained unconsciousness**. She provides the nurtured soil that allows imaginative actions to occur. The High Priestess represents our unrealized **potential** and waiting for a lively attitude to bring it to fruition. It is important to know that the expression of negative and positive does not directly connect to good and bad. Human distinctions like good and bad do not directly relate to the tarot. The Magician and the High Priestess are 100 percent equal in both importance and value to the deck. Each card is important to bring balance to the Fool. It is common to view the pessimistic as darkness following our existence, but without the shadow, we would not be able to experience the light that comes with positivity. We also would not be able to create the positivity if we did not have the ground cultivated for potential.

Through growth, the Fool is able to become more and more aware of the surroundings around them. It is common with most babies to first recognize their **Mother**. This is the loving and warm woman who nurtures and cares for them. The Fool will also come to understand Mother Earth, who is the nurturer in a bigger sense of the term. The Empress (3) is the representation of the world of the natural world and feeling. A baby learns delight through exploring situations through senses like touch, taste, and smell. A baby does not get tired of the sounds and sights that allow his senses to bloom. It is natural for one to enjoy the **abundant** decency of Mother Earth. This is how she surrounds us with her support. Without Mother Earth, our senses would not be ignited early on in our lives and we would not have the opportunity to relish in the goodness that she provides. Without the support of the mother, the Fool is likely to not succeed in the journey through life.

The next individual the Fool encounters is the Emperor (4), or the Father form. The Father represents **authority** and **structure**. As the baby leaves the arms of the mother to explore the world, it will soon realize the patterns that are to emerge. Substance reacts in ways that can be predicted and make it possible to travel around. There is a new kind of pleasure the child experience when it is exposed to the idea of order. This is when the Fool also encounters **rules**. The Fool will learn that their will is not supreme, but there will be definite behaviors that are essential to continue to care for their well-being. The Fool will understand that there are people who are the authority and they will enforce these guidelines. The restrictions may be frustrating for the Fool in the beginning, but the Father will provide patient direction and the Fool will begin to comprehend their reason in the human race.

With age, ultimately the Fool will venture out of the house of its parents and into the wider world. The culture will expose the Fool to its beliefs and traditions, which will begin the official **education** process. The Hierophant (5) represents the prearranged **belief systems** that inform and enclose a growing child in society. A Hierophant is a person who can interpret information and concealment that are considered secret. On the fifth card, we see a spiritual shape blessing two different acolytes. It is possible that he is bringing them into church association. Even though this image is considered spiritual, it is really a representation for all types of initiations. At the step, the child is taught in all the different aspects of humanity and becomes a part of its exacting society and understands the earth view. The Fool learns to recognize with a **group** and learns the good judgment of belonging. The Fool does enjoy learning the background of society and strives to show how sound he can **conform** to them.

Once older, ultimately the Fool will face two brand new tests. They will experience a powerful push for **sexual** encounters with one more individual. Before this experience, the Fool is typically only self-concerned. Now they will feel a balance tendency, to reach out to another person and become half of a complete affectionate partnership. The Fool will yearn for a **relationship** that is represented in the Lovers (6). This is also the time for the Fool to decide what it **believes on its own**. It is good enough to conform to society while the Fool is still learning and growing, but at this point, they must decide their individual **values** to ensure they are true to themselves. This is when the Fool will begin to question the opinions that are received.

By the time that the Fool becomes fully developed, they have a well-built identity and can be considered to have a mastery over itself. Through **willpower** and discipline, there is a growth of internal control which allows the Fool to work over the surroundings. The Chariot (7) represents the dynamic personality and that is the Fool's highest accomplishment at this point in the journey. On the 7th card that represents the Chariot, there is an illustration of a confident strong figure riding **victoriously** through its own humankind. There is a sense of **visible control** of themselves and everything that they observe. For instance, the Fool's forceful victory is all that it might desire at the time, and he feels self-approval certainly. They are declared self-assurance of adolescence.

Over moments in time, the Fool will be presented with fresh challenges from life. These challenges will cause suffering and disenchantment. They have a lot of occurrences to portray the value of **Strength** (8). They are pushed to build up bravery and determination and to find the mind to keep pushing forward in spite of the delays that are thrown at them in all instances of life. The Fool also finds out the silent qualities of acceptance and patience. They realize the headstrong authority of the Chariot must be calmed down by kindness and the **softer power** of an affectionate approach. Oftentimes, strong obsessions can float up, just as soon as the Fool has considered as though they have everything, including them, under control.

Soon, the Fool will be led to ask "Why?" which is an age-old question. They will become engrossed with a new desire to **search** for understanding, not just out of inquisitiveness, but out of a deep feeling to discover things like why people are alive, if they are to only be ill with and ultimately pass away. The Hermit (9) represents the want to find a deeper reality. The Fool at this point will begin to **look inward**, trying to comprehend the stance and inspirations they experience. The bodily world holds less magnetism to the Fool, and there are instances where they will seek **solitude** away from a chaotic civilization. In time they may appear to search out a **guide or teacher** who can give counsel and offer a course on how to carry on through existence.

After soul searching for a long period of time, the Fool begins to realize and see how everything connects to one another. They have a **vision** of the world's phenomenal drawing, with all of its complicated cycles and patterns. The Wheel of Fortune (10) is a symbol of the unexplained world, with all of its parts working together in agreement. Once the Fool is able to view the world's beauty and everything working in order, even if it is just for a brief amount of time, the Fool then realizes that they are able to find some of the answers they are looking for. For the Fool, it sometimes seems as though everything is working by the action of fate. A miraculous occurrence or a chance encounter begins to process this change. The Fool may or may not begin to realize their **destiny** in the succession of events that lead him or her to this **turning point** in their life. Because they had been in solidarity, they feel ready for **movement** and activity again at this point. They have a wider perspective and can see himself or herself within the bigger picture of a worldwide plan. The feeling of function that the Fool once felt is eventually restored.

Now is the time for the Fool to understand what the vision means to them personally. They are now looking back on their life and tracing all of the **cause and effect** relationships that have brought the Fool through life up until this point. They are able to take **responsibility** for their past actions so that they are able to make amends and ensure that they are going to follow a more truthful route in the upcoming. The demands of Justice (11) must be served so that they are able to wipe their slate clean and begin again. The encounter is a time of **decision** for the Fool. This is a time that calls for making important choices. The question that arises is: Will the Fool remain true to their insights or will they allow themselves to trip back into an easier and supremely ignorant continuation that does not allow for future growth?

The Fool does not feel daunted at this point and pushes forward on into life. The Fool is feeling a sense of determination to realize their vision, and finding out that life is not as easy to tame as they once believed. Sooner or later, the Fool will encounter an internal cross – an understanding that can be considered too complicated to tolerate. This devastating test will soon humble the Fool until they realize that there is no other option than to give up and **let go** of the control they wanted. It is natural at first for the Fool to feel defeated and lost. The fool will feel as though they have **given up** everything, but from the depths of the inner self, they will learn the truth. They find that when they let go of the struggle they feel to be in control, everything will have the opportunity to work as it should. The Fool becomes open and susceptible and finds the support of their Inner Self. The Fool learns to give in to the experience of life, as opposed to trying to fight them all the time. There is a surprising level of joy felt, as life begins to have a manageable flow. The Fool will begin to feel **suspended** in an eternal moment. They will feel free of urgency and pressure. The truth, however, is that their world has been turned the wrong way up. The Fool is now the Hanged Man (12), apparently suffering for a cause, but is actually calm and at tranquility.

At this point in their life, the Fool will begin to **eliminate** old behavior and worn out advancements. The will begin to remove all nonessential elements because they are able to appreciate the fundamentals of life. They will go through **endings** as they put the older aspects of life behind them. The procedure may seem like a part of them is dying because it is the death (13) of what they know to be familiar to them that now allows for the growth of a new person. At the time, it can be seen that this **inexorable change** seems to be overwhelming the Fool, but ultimately, they will rise up to find out that not all death is a lasting state. It is simply a **transition** to new, and a more satisfying way of living life.

Now that the Fool has embraced the Hermit the Fool has been swinging forward and back on an emotional swing. Now, they realize that **temperance** (14) is what a **balancing** stability feels like. They are able to discover their true poise and feel a sense of equilibrium. The Fool experiences the extremes and is now able to appreciate things that come in self-control. The fool has now pooled all aspects of the self into a centered entire person that glows with **health** and a sense of happiness. How elegant and supple is the angel on Card 14 in comparison to the influential but unbending ruler in the Chariot? The fool has come a very long way in realizing the feelings of a pleasant-sounding life.

At this point in life, the Fool has their graceful composure, peaceful mind, and their health. There really is not much more they could need. It can be said that on everyday terms, there is not much more needed, but the Fool is brave and continues to follow the deepest levels of their life form. In this state, the Fool will soon come face to face with the Devil (15). Contrary to popular belief, the devil is not an evil menacing presence that resides external of us. The Devil can be seen as the combination of **ignorance** and **hopelessness** that we feel inside us. The seductive magnetism of the **material** world connects us so that we frequently do not even understand that we are a topic of a slave to them. We continue through life on an incomplete diversity of knowledge and supremely ignorant of the magnificent earth that is home to our factual legacy. The duo on Card 15 can often be seen as chained together. They could easily free themselves but they do not even take in for questioning their **bondage**. They look like the Lovers, but they are uninformed that their love is restricted within a thin array. The price of this lack of knowledge is an inner center feeling of gloom.

How does the Fool remove them from the devil? Is it possible to come out from underneath his influence? It is possible that the Fool can only find a sense of **liberation** through the **unexpected change** that is shown by the Tower (16). The Tower is the personality castle each one of us has built approximately in our inner center. Imagine this fortress as grey, cold, and rock hard. It seems as though it is protecting but it is actually more like a prison. Sometimes it takes an intense moment of crisis to generate enough strength to break down the stockade of the Tower. On card 16, we can see a bright bolt of lightning hitting the building. It has removed the people that are within the Tower and they appear to be **falling** to their death. The crown shows that they were at one time rulers who were proud of their positions but now they are modest by the power that is stronger than they are. The Fool might need this strong shift in direction to be able to free them, but it is the resultant **revelation** that makes the excruciating experience valuable. The gloomy anguish is wrenched away in a second, and the glow of the truth is free to stand out downward onto the Fool.

The Fool then feels a sense of **serene** tranquil. The happy imagery that is on the Star (17) card show to its sense of calm. The lady pictured on Card 17 is nude as though her spirit is no longer concealed behind a type of costume. Big stars stand out in a clear sky serving as a spokesperson of **optimism** and **motivation**. The Fool is now blessed with a faith that is completely replacing the unconstructive energies of the Devil. They have trust in themselves and their faith in the future is restored. They are overflowing with delight and have one wish to share it **charitably** with the rest of the earth. The Fool's spirit is open, and they pour out their love generously to everyone and everything. This quiet after the storm is an exciting instant for the Fool.

Now is the time for this ideal calm to experience an upset. What could cause this and create another challenge for the Fool? It is this emotion of calm that makes the Fool susceptible, and likely fall for the **illusions** of the Moon (18). The joy that the Fool feels is within a feeling state. Their positive emotions are not yet examined in mind clearness. In this dreamlike state, the Fool is vulnerable to daydream and a fake picture of reality. The Moon stimulates the imaginative **mind**. It opens the method for wonderful and odd judgment to rise awake from the subconscious, but deep-seated **doubts** and anxieties will also turn up. These moments of experiences may cause the Fool to suffer misplaced and **dazed**.

It is the clearness of the Sun (19) that directs the Fool's sense of mind. The Sun's light shines a light on all the concealed places. It dispels the clouds of fear and confusion. It **enlightens** so the Fool is able to feel and understand the goodness that is in the world. Now the Fool enjoys a lively power and sense of eagerness. The Star's honesty has solidified into a wild promise. The Fool is the nude baby pictures on Card 19, moving out delightfully to face a new daytime. No confrontation is too much of a challenge for the Fool. The Fool feels a beaming **strength**. They become involved in impressive activities as they draw everything they need to themselves. They are able to recognize their magnitude.

The Fool has once again been **reborn**. Their fake, ego-self has been gotten rid of, allowing a true self that is radiant to manifest. They have discovered that joy, and not fear, is the center of life. The Fool feels **absolved**. They forgive themselves and they forgive others, knowing that their real self is pure and can be considered good. They may regret the mistakes of their past, but they know they were due to the ignorance of their true nature. They can at the present choose to feel washed and start again. It is time for the Fool to make a deeper **Judgment** (20) about existence. This is an individual day of calculation for the Fool. Since they now see themselves truly, they can make the necessary decisions that are required for their future. They can choose intelligently which principles to treasure and which of those they can get free of. The cherub on Card 20 is the Fool's Higher Self **asking** them to rise up and fulfill the guarantee of a full life. They discover their true trade or their motivation for inflowing into existence. Doubt and hesitation disappear, and they are prepared to go after their dream.

The Fool now enters the World (21) again, but on this occasion is with a total understanding. They have **included** all of the unequal fractions of themselves and have successfully attained completeness. They have reached a fresh level of contentment and life **completion**. The Fool experiences life as filled and significant. The future is infinite and filled with guarantee. In line with their individual vocation, they will become actively **involved** in the happenings of the world. They render service by sharing their exclusive gifts and aptitudes. They will find that they prosper at whatever they are willing to attempt. Because they act from their sense of inner confidence, the whole world works together to see that their efforts are to be rewarded. Their **undertakings** are many.

So, as you can see, the Fool's journey through life was not at all foolish. Through persistence and sincerity, they are able to reestablish the impulsive course that first encouraged them on their look for self, but now they are completely aware of their position in the earth. The cycle is formally over, but the Fool will never stop rising. Soon, they will be ready to start a new trip that will lead them to even better levels of accepting. Then the cycle repeats itself. This will happen over the course of the Fool's lifetime.

CHAPTER 3
The Minor Arcana

Since we now know that the Major Arcana expresses what can be considered as worldwide thesis, the Minor Arcana brings those themes downward into sensible areas to show how they function in daily events. The minor arcana is known to represent the worry, behavior, and feelings that create the drama of our everyday lives. There are known to be 56 cards in the minor arcana and they are comprised of 4 different suits. These suits are labeled as Wands, Cups, Swords, and Pentacle. Each of these ensembles is known to stand for a scrupulous move toward a life occasion.

Wands

The wands are the suit known to be the suit of originality, action, and progress. They are linked with qualities such as eagerness, adventure, self-assurance, and threat taking. The suit of the Wand corresponds to the yang or the manly principle in Chinese attitude and is also known to be associated with the element of Fire. A flame that continuously flickers is a perfect symbol to represent the force of the Wand. The energy of the Wand pours externally and generates fervent participation.

The meaning of the Wand cards deal with a religious level of awareness and reflect what is important to a person at the central part of their life form. Wand cards speak to what makes you tick, your personality, your ego, enthusiasm, self-concept, and your personal energy. The personal energy is both internal and what is expressed externally. There are negative aspects that are attributed to the wand cards. These include elements of fantasy, egotistical behavior, spontaneity, a lack of purpose or direction, and a feeling of worthlessness. Wand cards are also representations of the astrological symbols that represent fire. These astrological symbols are Leo, Sagittarius, and Aries. If you see a Wand card in a tarot spread reading, it often relates to a person who is a Leo, Sagittarius, or Aries star sign. Wand people experience characteristics such as energetic, charismatic, spiritual, and warm. If a tarot reading is showing to be mostly Wand cards, you can be certain that you are looking for answers to issues that are mainly based on thought, or that these are the first stages of development for the issue at hand. You may also be seeking a greater purpose and meaning in your life and will want to understand more about what energizes and motivates a person. There are 13 Wand cards in the suit.

Cups

The Cup cards are the suit of emotional and spiritual existence. The Cup cards describe our inner states, feelings, and patterns that emerge in our relationships. The energy of this suit is known to flow inward. The suit of Cups corresponds to the yin or the womanly principle in Chinese viewpoint. They are also linked with the element of Water. Water has the aptitude to run and fill in the voids within spaces and to maintain and mirror on changing moods makes it the perfect symbol to represent the Cups suit. The element of water is emblematic of variability, outlook and emotions, relationships, emotions, healing, and purification. It is a womanly element and reflects the slight authority that frequently is held in most women. It is open, purifying, flexible, and graceful. In a deck of playing cards, Cups are representations of the Hearts.

Cups cards typically show that you are working through something with your heart and not your head. This then reflects your impulsive responses and your routine reaction to circumstances. Cups are also linked to imagination, fantasy, idealism, and creativity. The negative aspects of the Cups suit include being completely disengaged and dispassionate, overly emotional or having impractical outlooks, and fantasizing about what could be. There is usually powerlessness to truly express yourself, repressed emotions, and a lack of originality. Cup cards represent the astrological signs of water. These signs are Pisces, Cancer, and Scorpio. When you see a Cups card in a tarot pull reading, it often relates to a person who is a Pisces, Cancer, or Scorpio star sign. Cups people are generally emotional, artistic, creative, and humane. They are connected with their emotional self and will draw energy from what they are feeling within. If a tarot card reading is mostly Cups cards, you are seeking solutions to what are primarily emotional conflicts, love matters, personal interactions, creativity, and feelings. There are 14 Cups cards in the suit.

Swords

The Swords are considered to be the suit of intelligence, thought, and reason. They are concentrated on justice, fact, and moral principles. Swords cards are also known to be associated with the element of Air. A symbol of mental clarity such as a cloudless sky that is filled with light and open is the Swords cards idyllic. This suit is also linked with feelings that lead to unhappiness and a lack of harmony. Our intelligence is a precious benefit, but as a manager of ego, it can guide us off route if it is not concentrated with the wisdom of our Inner Guide.

Swords are often seen as being doubled edged and, in this way, the Suit of Swords symbolizes the fine balance between power and intelligence and how these two elements can be put forth for either good or evil depending on the person. As such, the Swords must stay unbiased by spirit, the Wands cards, and feeling, the Cups cards, to have the most positive effect on a person. The element of Air that the Swords are associated with is seen as intangible and unseen. It is also known to be in steady movement. Air can be unnoticed and mostly still, but can easily become a whipping wind or a forceful breeze. It is authoritative but also stimulating. The air element can relate to action, knowledge, change, and power. It is a manly energy that can lead by power or force, even though it will remain hidden. If you are relating Swords in a deck of playing cards, they would represent the Spades.

The Sword tarot card suit definitions are linked with change, force, power, action, oppression, conflict, ambition, and courage. Action can be both destructive and constructive. The negative aspects of the Sword tarot cards include harsh judgment, a lack of sympathy, anger, guilt, and spoken and cerebral abuse. Swords represent the astrological signs of Air, Aquarius, Libra, and Gemini. When you see a Sword Court Card in a tarot card spread, it often relates to a person with an Aquarius, Libra, or Gemini star sign. Swords people are generally clever, thoughtful, balanced, rational, and outstanding communicators. They are also rational people and like to indulge the world by understanding and analyzing what is going on around them. On the opposite side, Swords people can be domineering, cruel, rigid, and challenging.

If you see mostly Swords cards in a tarot card spread, you are seeking solutions to what is first and foremost psychological struggles, arguments, and conflicts or decisions that have to be complete. Also, there could be a lot of urging or even a presence of aggression. While Swords carry with them many pessimistic or forceful and burly messages, Swords serve as a warning to be more careful of what is happening around you in your present life. There are 14 Swords cards in the deck.

Pentacles

The Pentacles are known as the suit of security, common sense, and material concerns. The Pentacles are also associated with the element of Earth and the tangible necessities of working with substance. In Pentacles, we commemorate our interactions with animals and plants, the beauty of nature, and the bodily experiences that we have in the body. Pentacles also represent affluence and wealth of all kinds. Often, this suit is also referred to as Coins, which is an obvious sign of the swap of services and goods within the physical world that we live in. The suit of Pentacles deals with the outside level of awareness and mirrors the outer situations of your finances, creativity, work, and health. What we make of our outer surrounding is what they have to do with and how we create it, transform it, shape it, and grow it. On a mysterious level, Pentacles are commonly associated with self-image, self-esteem, and ego.

The element of Earth is tangible, earthy, and touchable. It creates the groundwork which the earth can produce and expand, and it nurtures and supports the trees and all other plants. Earth is stable, supportive, grounded, and fertile. It is a womanly element that is receptive as it takes in nutrients and rays of the sun and then uses that energy to maintain the life that grows out of it. In a deck of playing cards, the Pentacles are associated with Diamonds.

Pentacle tarot card means material parts of life which includes business, work, money, trade, property, and other material possessions. The positive aspects of the Pentacle suit cards include prosperity, proof, realization, and manifestations. The negative aspects of the Pentacle suit include being gluttonous and overly money-oriented, jealousy, over-indulging and not willing to exercise, being unable to effectively manage money, and being overly paying attention on a career to the disadvantage of other life priorities. In order to counteract these negative effects, you must return to the natural world to root yourself and rediscover what is truly significant to you.

Pentacles tarot cards often represent the astrological signs associated with Earth. These star signs include Taurus, Virgo, and Capricorn. If you see a Pentacles court card in a tarot card spread, it often relates to a person who is a Taurus, Virgo or Capricorn star sign. Pentacles people are generally career-minded, practical, generous, and down-to-earth. They are tactile people who like the experiences of a tangible physical world. They are connected through the senses and seek pleasurable and sometimes indulgent experiences. If you see a tarot card spread that is mostly comprised of Pentacles cards, you are seeking solutions to what are primarily material conflicts, concerns with career or work, and financial matters.

Each minor arcana has a distinct quality. Everyday experiences of ours are a combination of these four different ways of going about it. Your tarot card readings will show how the different energies are positively or negatively impacting your life, at any particular moment. The suits are pre-arranged very similar to a standard deck of playing cards. There are number cards, which range from an Ace card to the number Ten. There are also four court cards which range from King, Queen, Knight, and Page. Each of these cards has a unique position to play in presenting how its energy in the world is expressed.

Aces

An Ace is known to announce the theme of a suit. An Ace always represents positive energy. It is the one thing that represents the best its suit has to offer. There are four Aces of tarot. They are all bright, beautiful blessings brimming with optimism and potential. Simply, Aces are the beginning of the numbered cards. It can act as a one but is not at the same time. When we take into account all of the details and symbolism that lies in each and every one of the 78 cards in a tarot deck, it should not be taken lightly that Aces are not called card number one.

In most instances, Aces are more likely to represent zeros. It is a seed rooted in potential. Relate it to a seed that is planted underground, it is waiting for its moment to sprout, a sign of potential of what happens next, and something that has yet to be fully brought to life. Within tarot reading, aces show us possibility. It is ultimately up to us to turn something into something more than what it was originally. To most, an Ace card can be seen as a pure form of energy. Much like a seed in the ground it is, before they have actually turned into something. Let us now examine the Aces and the energy they bring. We will also see what you can do with the energy it brings to bring more of it into your life and call in more of that potential into your life.

Middle Cards

Each of the middle cards is numerical cards that present a different feature of each suit. The Wants travel around themes such as personal power (2), leadership (3), excitement (4), and competition (5). A card might present the idea from more than a few dissimilar ways. The Five of Pentacles shows the many faces of want. These are hard times, usually materials wants, poor health, a physical want to get healthy, and dismissal, which is an emotional want to be loved and accepted.

Tens Cards

These cards can be seen as the conclusion or finish of an event, undertaking, or a cycle. They represent both the end as well as the stages of a new beginning in its early development. The Tens can be seen as being full of happenings and meanings. The easiest way to see the tens is by using the idea of 3 C's. The three C's are culmination, completion, and complexity. Tens represent the maximum expression of the suit. In one card, you will see all the events, experiences, and lessons.

Court Cards

The Court cards are depicted as people with the characteristics that reflect the character of their grade and suit. The court cards show us convinced ways of people being on the earth so that a person can use those styles when suitable. It also shows us when to avoid them. The Court Cards are represented by a King, Queen, Knight, and a Page card. Court cards are most often the hardest cards to interpret. This is because there are so many different ways to interpret each card. You can interpret them as people, personalities, or as situations, and even more.

- A King card is a grown-up and manly card. He is a person or personality of an achiever and his focus is towards the outward events of life. The King card is a demonstration of power, control, and the completeness of some areas associated with the King card suit. The style of a King card can be seen as strong, assertive, and very direct. The King Card is working with the outcome and sensible, how-to matters.

- A Queen card is also grown-up but a womanly card. She symbolizes the traits of her specific suit, rather than physically acting them out like the King card. The focus of the Queen card is inward instead of outward. Her style is typically tranquil and innate. A Queen card is less concerned with results than the enjoyment of just being a part of the world. The Queen is associated with relationships, feelings, and self-expression.

- A Knight card represents a young adolescent. The Knight is not able to express himself with a level of balance. The Knight is known to vary wildly between one extreme to another, typically with emotions, as the Knight tries to relate to the world in a successful way. A Knight is known to be in the world of excess. He is also seen as sincere and eager, which are redeeming qualities against the other personality traits of the Knight. The reader can delight in the Knight's spirit and level of energy.

- A Page card is the representation of a playful child. A Page physically acts the qualities of his suit. These qualities are acted out with abandon and pleasure from the Page. The Page's approach is easy, loose, and spontaneous. It does not go very deep into self-expression. The Page is a symbol of adventure and possibility.

CHAPTER 4
Imagery Symbolism In The Cards

Even as a person just beginning their tarot journey, it is easy to understand that tarot cards are extremely rich in imagery symbolism. If you understand the symbols on the cards, you should be able to offer a full tarot reading in the interpretation of those symbols, even if you are not completely sure of each meaning of the individual cards. Depending on your tarot deck, symbols can come from many different ways from the cards. Symbols come from numerology, meanings of colors, archetypal energies, astrology, and spiritual symbolism. If you ever find yourself stuck on the significance of a card in a specific card pull, you can refer to the card's symbols to provide more information.

Major Arcana Tarot Symbolism

There are 22 major arcana cards in a typical tarot card deck. Each of the major arcana cards contains symbolism based on numerology and archetypes. The major arcana cards are known to be numbered from 0 to 21 using roman numerals. They depict the soul's journey from birth, newness, and innocence, to adult and enlightenment.

- The Fool: innocence, the beginning of a journey through life
- The Magician: conception, alchemy
- The High Priestess: subconscious, instinct
- The Empress: compassion, wise woman, feminine
- The Emperor: power, authority, masculine
- The Hierophant: spiritual guidance
- The Lovers: partnerships, relationships
- The Chariot: goals, motivation, ambition
- Strength: perseverance, courage, standing up to life's challenges
- The Hermit: going within to find your personal wisdom
- Wheel of Fortune: change, impermanence
- Justice: balance, fairness
- The Hanged Man: perspective, patience

- Death: endings, change, new beginnings
- Temperance: moderations
- The Devil: lack of control, temptation
- The Tower: catastrophic change
- The Star: encouragement, healing, hope
- The Moon: deep fears or emotions, reflection, subconsciousness
- The Sun: awakening, excitement, happiness, joy
- Judgment: righting past mistakes, taking stock, recognizing your past actions' effects on others
- The World: fulfillment, the end of a cycle or journey

Symbols of the Minor Arcana

As we know from previous chapters, there are 56 cards that make what is known as the Minor Arcana in the tarot card deck. They are divided into suits that are similar to an average deck of playing cards. The suits of the minor arcana are the pentacles, wands, cups, and swords. The meanings of each of these suits represent each of the four classic elements. These elements are earth, air, fire, and finally water.

Pentacles Symbolism

As we remember, Pentacles represent the element of earth. This element is grounded, rooted in the physical being. When a pentacle card appears in a tarot spread, it is a reflection of information on the seeker's physical state, or it could be discussing information about the physical world the person is currently living in. It is possible for a Pentacles card to address the following topics:

- Finances
- Health
- Property
- Business or trade
- Career

Symbolism Associated with Cups

For a refresher, Cups represent the element of water. One easy way to remember this is that a cup is used to hold water. Water is the emotional element, so when a cups card appears in your tarot card spread, it is referring to issues that are primarily dealing with the emotions. It is likely pulling a Cups card is addressing the following topics:

- Emotions and feelings
- Relationships and love
- Connections with others
- Creative endeavors
- Personal interactions

Wands Symbolism

Wands represent the element known as fire. A tip to remember is to think about sparks shooting out of the end of a magic wand like you sometimes see in the movies. Fire is an active and primal energy that is associated with higher thought and spirituality. It is also known to be representative of passion and drive. When wands show up in a tarot card reading spread, it is likely indicating some of the following ideas:

- Goals and ambitions
- Purpose
- Passion and drives
- Motivation and meaning
- Change

Symbolism Associated with Swords

Finally, the suit of Swords represents the element of air. There is an easy way to remember this one. Think of slicing a sword through the air when in the middle of a battle. Air is known to be associated with your mental self and the realm of thought. When a Swords card shows up in your tarot reading, it is likely representing one of the following ideas:

- Confrontation
- Challenges
- Decisions
- Conflicts and arguments
- Courage

Symbolism of Numbers in Tarot Cards

A tarot card deck is very similar to a regular deck of playing cards. Each minor arcana tarot card is either a numbered card or a court card. Each of these cards has its own symbolic meaning in the tarot world.

- 1 (ace): new beginnings, unity
- 2: partnership, balance, relationships, duality
- 3: creativity
- 4: stability, structure
- 5: change, conflict, growth
- 6: harmony
- 7: growing spiritually, life lessons
- 8: understanding and accomplishments
- 9: success, coming to the end of a cycle or journey
- 10: completion, enlightenment

Court Card Symbolism in the Minor Arcana

The court cards are the face cards in each suit of the tarot. There are four court cards in each one of the four suits. Each one of the court cards represent the following in their suit:

- Page: service, youthful energy
- Knight: moving forward, taking action, mature energy
- Queen: compassion, empathy
- King: success, leadership, attainment

Colors Can Be Symbolic on Tarot Cards

All decks of tarot cards are unique but they all do have one characteristic in common, they are all extremely colorful. The colors chosen in the images on the tarot cards tend to have a symbolic meaning. These colors chosen are based on the psychological effects of the colors and the spiritual energy that is associated with auras and chakras. So when you are reading your tarot cards in a spread and interpreting their meaning, pay close attention to the colors the artist has chosen along with the images and numbers represented on the card.

- Silver: emotion, empathy, crown chakra, sensitivity
- White: newness, inexperience, birth, higher self, crown chakra
- Blue: communication, sadness, trust, judgment and criticism, throat chakra, peace, self-expression
- Purple: reason, critical thinking, third eye chakra, spirituality, intuition, psychic ability
- Green: healing, harmony, love, balance, bitterness, envy, heart chakra
- Yellow: spontaneity, enthusiasm, opportunity, solar plexus chakra
- Gold: spiritual leadership, divinity, mastery, crown chakra or above
- Orange: creative ideas, optimism, joy, sacral chakra
- Brown: comfort, neutrality, stability, earthiness, muddiness or lack of boundaries, sacral chakra

- Pink: forgiveness, compassion, femininity, love, heart chakra
- Red: safety, security, passion, anger, groundedness, root chakra
- Black: protection darkness or missing elements, illness, protection, negativity, root chakra

Associated Symbols of Art and Imagery on Tarot Cards

As you will come to see, most tarot cards have very detailed artwork on each card for an illustration of what the card represents. There are additional elements within the scene depicted on the card that will lead the reader to interpret the insights that should be gathered during a reading. More often than not, many of these elements are not what they appear to be, but they are symbolic and may have a different meaning than what appears to be obvious in the picture.

- Angels: inspiration, pay attention to details, listen to the inner voice
- Blindfold: someone is hiding the truth, someone is refusing to acknowledge the truth, seeker not seeing clearly
- Cat: unseen energy, be aware of all circumstances before acting, psychic ability
- Dog: heading in the right direction, truth, loyalty, honestly
- Flag: major change coming, pay attention
- Grapes: abundance, fertility
- Hammer: vocation, completing a task, use force to bring a chore to an end
- Ice: isolation, separation, growth through a complete season
- Keys: opportunity, discovery, knowledge
- Lizard: conscious effort yields big results, vision
- Ocean: Possibility, movement, emotion/states of emotion, relax and allow the power of the universe to work in your life
- Moon: the passing of time, change, reflection, femininity
- Pillar: support, seek a balanced solution, balance
- Rain: cleansing, sadness, opportunities for growth

- Ship: staying afloat, transformation, personal journey
- Tree: Strength, shelter, regeneration
- Wreath: Victory, triumph

Collective vs. Individual Wisdom

The first thing you will want to remember when looking into the symbolic meanings of the cards is that there is dissimilarity between communal knowledge and your own personal link to the ciphers. Collective wisdom is defined as being the commonly held associates for symbols passed down through traditional belief systems. Personal wisdom is defined as the individual associates that are formed through our own personal experiences. Let us take a look at an example to get a better understanding of the differences between these two definitions.

Example: A Circle

There is a commonly held meaning for a circle to represent the idea of cycles or eternal life. However, as an individual, you may have a different understanding of what a circle means. It might create an entirely different meaning or bring up a different memory for you rather than the thought of cycles or eternal life, and this is more than okay in the tarot world. Sometimes people may believe you have to learn the customary meanings of signs in the tarot, but you should always follow your own nature when you see a sign in a tarot spread. If all you know is the traditional meaning, then that's alright! If you need to make up your own in the moment, that's fine too! There is a way to incorporate both. You will want to start out with getting an understanding of what the customary meanings of the tarot symbols are but you can also infuse your own personal connections to those symbols at the same time.

Make the Most out of the Symbolism in Your Tarot Cards

Begin with what you are already aware of. When you are reading tarot, come from a place of confidence, even if it is your very first reading. For instance, if you are familiar and have an interest in Christian symbolism, think about these symbols and meaning and what you know about it. Think about how they are being shown through the tarot cards. This will give you a confidence boost while doing your reading. You do not need to sense like you have to study all fresh things and become an immediate subject matter expert at everything in order to appreciate the symbols in your tarot cards. Next, you can find familiar symbols and read more about their definitions. If you look through your deck and see that there are a few repeating images or symbols across the cards, look up the meaning of the symbol and how it can be represented across multiple cards. For instance, there are a bunch of landscape images in tarot cards. Looking into this meaning can be really helpful to find out the collective wisdom around this symbol. What can a landscape scene traditional mean? You can also explore your personal connections with symbols that are represented in the tarot. This is where enjoyable aspects of tarot come in! You can truly use your instinct and start to attach more with your intuition when you try this method. Using a fortress as an example, this customary meaning is a place that is fairly secure, because there are walls all around the castle and it is very big and sturdy. You, however, might look at the castle and see the walls and think of a lack of liberty. So that might actually have a negative suggestion for you. It is a good workout to see what the castle truly means to you. Think about how you see a castle and how it differs from the collective wisdom of what a castle represents. You will also want to compare the symbols across the tarot cards. We can stick with the castle example. Pull out all the tarot cards that have a castle illustrated on them. Answer the following questions and evaluate how they differ from card to card:

- Does the connotation of a castle change as you look across the different cards?
- Are you standing inside the walls of the castle, or are you outside the walls?
- Do you feel excluded or included?
- Do you feel safe or unsafe?

- What is happening around the castle?
- Are castles really as powerful as you think they might be?

When you do this workout, you will start to see that dissimilar signs can take on different meanings. This depends on the situation of the card itself. There are two more ways you can begin to see symbolism differently. Now that you are fairly confident in the symbolism you are aware of, start to become more aware of different symbolism in different cultural contexts. You could also look into reading more about mythology. It is rich in symbolism and very easy to connect into your tarot practice. Once you have become a master at doing all of this research, it is wise to begin keeping a notepad of the symbols that you are discovering and mark down what each of them means to you. There is a beauty in this that you are no longer exclusively relying on what an important person tells you a symbol represents. You are going to begin to grow your personal experience around all of these symbols and make connections that are truly unique to you.

CHAPTER 5
Detailed Card Descriptions: Major Arcana

In this section, we will go over every detailed description of all of the cards you will encounter in the Major Arcana on your tarot journey. By now, you should have a basic understanding of the cards and their symbolism, but we will now begin to get even deeper into the cards and what they stand for. This will help you in your journey through tarot reading and eventually, you will be able to know all of the cards without having to look them up from your references. You should be able to know what the card means, the universal symbolism, as well as influencing your own symbolism meaning when you are done with this chapter and this book. For now, since you are still new to the practice, feel free to reference this chapter through your readings as often as you feel necessary until you are comfortable enough in your practice to go out on your own.

The World Tarot Card Description

The World card in a tarot card deck usually includes a moving figure in the middle. The dancing person on the card has one leg crossed over the other and holds wands in both hands. She symbolizes equilibrium and evolution in progress. The unity and fulfillment that she represents is not one that is stationary, but always altering, energetic, and undying.

The green garland of flowers that surrounds the middle figure symbolizes a level of achievement, while the red ribbons that wrap around the top and bottom of the wreath are symbolizing time without end. There are four things in each corner of the card as well. They are the same ones that are in the Wheel of Fortune card. These four figures represent Scorpio, Leo, Aquarius, and Taurus. They are representative of the four corners of the universe. Jointly, the four figures symbolize the agreement between all of their individual energies.

When the World card is pulled in your spread, it is an encounter of great accord and completeness. It symbolizes the progress when the outer and inner worlds become one single body. In some civilization, this state is described as illumination or paradise. There is an acknowledgment of the self that is intensely linked with all the other things and those we will all skip along the flow of life to one beat. Not only do you hear the cadence, but you add in it, including all of the valleys and peaks, the joys and sorrows that accompany it. The World card means fulfillment, completion, and achievement. This shows that all the efforts you are making are starting to pay off in your life. It reflects that you have just finished a major landmark and you are physically powerful enough to withstand any challenges you may face. The World could be a sign of completing a long-term project or any other major event in your life. It is possible for it to also mean the birth of a child, a marriage, commencement from school or anything else of great success. The World card shows that you have a wish to give back to the community. You have an obligation to make the world you live in an improved place because you have a belief that everything in it is connected.

If you pull the World card and it is reversed or upside down, it means that you are drawing near to something that shows an indication of the end of a journey. You may have been experiencing many happenings, but there is an odd feeling of emptiness that fills you when you look back on them as if all of the pieces have not yet come together. It is likely that you are not feeling closure although this event in your life has come to an end.

The Moon Tarot Card Description

When we are looking into the details of the Moon tarot card, you will notice that there is a path that leads all out into the distance. On either side of the path, there is a dog on one side and a wolf on the other side. They represent the animalistic nature of humans, one is domesticated and the other is feral and wild. There is also a crawfish close to the bottom of the card that is crawling out of the pond which the path seems to start from. In the far back distance, there stand two towers which the central path runs through, that are alluding to visible doubles in the card once again. All of the different elements of the card seem to reflect on it as if it is alluding to two different possibilities. When we walk down a path, we are walking a fine line between conscious and unconscious, or the fine line between a civilized dog and the forces of nature that are represented by the wolf on the other side. The two towards on opposing ends are representative of the forces of good and evil, and their similar appearance can allude to the difficulty that most humans face when they are trying to distinguish between the two.

If the Moon card is presented upright, the card can symbolize your imagination taking the best of you. If you are walking the path in the dark of night, you are taking a path that you are unsure of, as there could be danger lurking around in its depths. You are representative of the crawfish making its way onto and down the path. The light of the moon can bring you clarity and understand and this is a sign to trust and follow your intuition to guide you through the darkness. This is a reminder to be aware of the situations in your life that are causing fear and anxiety in your mind, whether it is currently happening or will happen in the future. It reminds you not to allow inner disturbances and self-deception to take the best of you. The deep fears and memories will need to be let go of, and the negative energies are to be released and turned into something constructive instead. The moon card can also be read as the existence of an illusion. There is a hidden truth to be discovered, for what you are seeing now might just be a trick of the light. You must begin your search for hidden forces that are waiting to be revealed.

If the Moon card is presented reversed or upside down, this reading can sometimes indicate there are darker and more negative aspects of the moon that are present in your life. It could be a representation of unhappiness or confusion. It is possible you want to make progress but you are not sure of what the right thing to do is. You will need to deal with your anxiety and fears to overcome them, for they are like the shadows of the moon in the dark night. It is time now to believe in yourself in order to move forward. The reversal of the Moon card will be able to also point out you are in an instinctive age or you have recently been in a battle with anxiety, confusion, and self-deception. It is also possible that you are misinterpreting how you have been feeling but you are at a point in which you are improving. Another revered moon can mean that the forces of the night that are bringing you the confusion you are feeling is starting to dissipate. You are now starting to manage your fear and anxiety. Whatever the negative energies are that you have been facing are slowly starting to fade away. It presents liberating experiences as you discover the positive side of the situation you are in.

The Devil Tarot Card Description

The Devil is represented in this card in his most well-known satyr form, otherwise known as Baphomet. This form of the devil is known as being half man and half goat. The devil also has wings like a bat and an inverted pentagram on his forehead. He is perched on a pedestal, which is chained to a man and woman who appear to be nude. This shows that he has domination over them. The man and the women in the image have horns, as if to show the more time that is spent with the devil, the less human they have become. The chains give the impression that the Devil is holding the man and woman captive. The man shows that he has a flame for his tail and the woman has a large bowl of grapes for her tail, which is a symbolization of their addiction to power and the finer things in life, respectively to each person. Looking a bit more closely, both the man and woman appear to be unhappy. Their individual power has been taking from them, and they are left exposed and ashamed in their outward nakedness.

If the Devil card appears to you in an upright position, this reading shows that you have feelings of emptiness, entrapment, and a lack of fulfillment in your life. It could also mean that you are feeling enslaved to materialism and opulence no matter how hard you try. You likely cannot shake off the feeling of wanting to indulge in luxurious living. You could already be well aware this lifestyle is leading you down a large rabbit hole, but you have a feeling that you are not able to control your actions or urges. Substance addiction or material pleasures can also be the reason why you have a feeling of powerlessness and entrapment. In situations such as these, you may feel almost like a slave to your impulses as you are unable to control them. You also may not feel like you have the willpower to direct yourself away from your addiction and toward something other than the satisfaction of your desires.

If the Devil card appears to you as reversed or upside down, the Devil card can be the moment when a person becomes self-aware and breaks all of the chains that come along with addiction and poor decision making. It might be because they are tired of running in circles and are in need of a change in lifestyle. One thing is usually clear with a reversed Devil card, breaking off the chains of addiction is never easy. A person has to be prepared to make the necessary changes that will initially seem painful but making the adjustments will pay off in the end by being able to become your true self again. A call to self-assessment is needed in this case as the individual needs to take some time and list all the things they need to get rid of in their life. Once this is done, then it would be time for the individual to embark on the journey of self-improvement.

The Hanged Man Description

The Hanged Man card shows a man who is poised upside down. He is shown to be lynching by one end from the living world tree. The tree roots are deep down into the world under the earth, and this tree is also known to hold up the heavens on top of the earth. It is whispered that the man is located like this on his own open determination. This is believed because the Hanged Man has a serene look on his appearance. His right foot is seen bound to the twigs of the tree but his left foot is obviously free. He is holding his hands behind his back in a way to depict his body as an inverted triangle. The red pants that he is wearing represent the bodily and human obsession, while the blue colored shirt that he wears represents tranquil emotions, a color mixture that is commonly seen on saints in other areas. His intellect is shown by the yellow color of the halo surrounding his head, the color of his hair, and the color of his shoes.

If the Hanged Man is presented upright, the Hanged man understands that his place is a forfeit that he needed to create in order to move onward. This means that the Hanged man needed to do repentance for past behavior or an intended step toward the back to shift his location on his path onward. The amount of time he spends here is not a wasted effort, he does this as part of the process in order to move forward. Being shown upside down can symbolize the feeling of walking a spiritual path because, in this moment, the world can be seen differently. When other people do not see or understand the need for sacrifice, you are able to see this situation differently. This is a natural course of action for you as you are walking the path alone. The Hanged Man is a representation of an action that needs to be suspended. This might indicate a certain period of indecision as a result. This means that certain decisions or actions which need to have a proper implementation are likely to be postponed even if there is a sense of urgency to act on this matter at this particular moment. Ultimately, it would be best if you are capable of stalling actions in order to ensure you have more time to reflect on making critical decisions. This card is used mainly to designate towards waiting and postponement. This suggests that this action might be something you need to commence in order to attain achievement or wait for the right chance for you to come along. Taking action is not always the right solution, and keep in mind that in certain cases, nonparticipation from action might transport you more benefits.

If the Hanged Man is presented reversed or upside down, it represents a very specific time or period during which you feel as if you are sacrificing a significant amount of time while you are not getting anything in return. You might have felt like certain things in your life are at a complete standstill without any particular conclusion or movement. It is as if you are putting your entire attention and effort into something but nothing turns out the way it should, or how you expected it to.

The Hermit Tarot Card Description

The Hermit shows an aged man standing unaccompanied at the peak of the mountain while holding a lamp in one of his hands and a stick on the other. The mountain indicates achievement, development, and accomplishment. The Hermit tarot card refers to the height of religious knowledge that he reached and that he is ready to pass on that information to everybody. There is also a strong obligation he has to his objective and a hard consciousness of the trail that he is taking. Inside the lamp, you will notice a star with 6 points which is also known as the Seal of Solomon. This symbol represents understanding. The stick that he holds depicts power and authority.

If the Hermit card is presented upright, this means that the Hermit is a seeker of knowledge that can only come from inside. A forlorn nomad on a path during the night, he looks for what can only be achieved through long periods of loneliness and separation, his inner voice. In order to hear it, he must cut off from the large crowds knowing that their voices and needs intimidate to overcome his own. He walks through the dark nighttime of his unaware mind, guided only by the dim light of the North Star, with his destination being his home, or more likely himself. It is very likely you are currently thinking through the idea that you need to be alone. Never be frightened to take this possibility to reflect, as it could always help you clear your mind of all the chaos that comes with daily life. The Hermit may also refer to your attempt in taking action that is unadulterated and allied with your true inner self. You are likely penetrating your inner soul for management on what is right, and where your subsequent steps are to be. The hermit making a manifestation in a reading can also symbolize the form of someone who will come to your life that will act as your adviser.

When the Hermit card is presented in a spread reverse or upside down, you are likely in a situation where you would prefer to be alone. There is nothing wrong with feeling this way. However, there is a likelihood that your separation may become harmful to both yourself and others. The Hermit sets forth with the best of meaning to search for his inner truth, his path innermost may also be filled with great danger. Going inward may lead to madness and the void, for the unaware is filled with ideas and pictures that the Hermit may not yet appreciate, lurking and waiting to entice you inside. Like a man that gets lost in his own dreams, the Hermit may find himself wedged in a world of his own, where he becomes very much alone and trapped. This world is unreal. You must learn that there is a need for balance between your need for reality with connection to your associated human. When in relation to your work, the Hermit reversed meaning refers to you being prepared to get to the foundation of something that has been bothering you for a long period of time now. There is much penetrating to be done, and it will be your duty to ask the question that will let the other citizens understand the state of affairs.

The Lovers Tarot Card Description

In the Lovers card, the woman and the man in the image are shown as being secluded and sanctified by a seraph above. The couple seems safe and content in their dwelling, which appears on the card to be the Garden of Eden. The tree with fruit with the snake behind the woman is an allusion to that biblical story, which tells of humanity's fall into enticement and into the realm of fleshy tissue and sensuality. The angel shown here is Raphael, who is the angel of air. He is the same constituent of the zodiac sign that is represented in this card, which is the Gemini. Air is linked with psychological activity, with the message being at the forefront, which is the groundwork for healthy and lasting relationships. His approval seems to give this card a sense of harmony and balance. The union symbolization appears to be in a majestic sense between two forces that are contrasting.

If the Lovers card is presented upright in a tarot card spread, it means that the main meaning within the Lovers is good looks, harmony, and excellence in a relationship. The connection that they have shaped is very strong, and it can show that the two are connected in matrimony, and it may also represent other close and cherished relationships if they are not nuptial. The faith and the harmony that the lovers have given each of them reassurance and power, in which they are encouraging the other.

Another meaning behind the Lovers card is that of the thought of choice. There is a choice between things that are mutually exclusive and opposing. This could mean of a tight spot that you need to think through cautiously and make the finest decision given your state. On a more individual level, the Lovers can be a symbol that can apply to individuals which are the development of your own character belief system, regardless of what are the standards of humanity. We see this as an expansion from the Hierophant, who made announcements and passed on his knowledge through a more commonly consistent system. This is one of the important times in someone's life when you take the time to figure out what you want to be standing up for, and what in your life your philosophy will truly be. To start, you must first make up your choice about what you find significant and inconsequential in every aspect of your life. You will want to be as truthful to yourself as possible, so you will be authentic and genuine to the people who are surrounding you and you share the most time with.

A Lovers card that is presented reversed or upside down will most likely point to both inner self and outer conflicts that you are going through. The dissonance can make daily life hard and it is likely that it could be putting unconstructive pressure on your relationships. It is important that you take a moment or two to think through about what you are hurting or grueling yourself for, so you can fix the issues or leave them be. During this time, you should also always be thinking about your belief system and your personal values to make sure that they are allied with what you want to happen from your life. A reversed Lovers card can also mean communication in disconnect. The groundwork for your relationships may be intermittent, creating an inequity between you and your partner or loved ones in your family. The unity normally present within the card has become unbalanced. The Lovers reversed can also point to that lately you have been avoiding accountability for your actions and their penalty. You could have made a decision that was based on your desire for instant fulfillment but are now blaming others around you for the penalty of the mistaken action that is now beginning to catch up to you. This is the time for you to need to say sorry for your mistakes and make compensation or make decisions that are better in the future and learn to let the past go.

The Empress Tarot Card Description

The Empress card shows a woman sitting alone on a chair that can be a throne. From the rich natural world that surrounds her, we can assume that this woman represents the Mother Earth, who is a fertility goddess. Venus rules her world which is a sign that there is complete harmony, love, luxury, and fertility giving by this goddess. The woman in the picture has blonde hair that is crowned with stars, which is a signal of her connection to the spiritual realm in a divine way. She is dressed in a patterned robe of pomegranates that represent fertility, and she is seated on seat cushions that are embroidered with a sign that is a representation of Venus. She is bounded by a charming and lush green forest with a river stream right through it. The Empress brings plenty to those she meets in a reading and many blessings.

The Empress presented in an upright position is a strong sign of pregnancy and motherhood. To confirm it, you can look for other tarot cards in a spread to see if the person is truly experiencing a pregnancy with motherly, nurturing, and caring personality signs. The Empress card could also mean the delivery of a new idea, project, or industry in your life. You can be sure that such situations and projects would end very successfully in your life, and you should know that owing to the good fortune that is brought with this card. Discover and bring onward those ideas that have been wedged in your brain and spirit and make sure that you dedicate yourself towards finishing them. This card is a sign that someone is going to be well taken care of and successful. As the archetype of the mother earth, the Empress is also an encouragement to spend time with nature, spending more time outside, and the mother of all of us.

If the Empress is presented reversed or upside down, this indicates that you have started placing too much concern and effort to other people's problems and have lost too much of your own willpower and strength. While the Empress's way of being is to shower her loved ones with attention and care, this can sometimes be too much, and she can go above and beyond. It is likely you might be smothering the ones you love with your well-intentioned actions while neglecting your own needs, which then turns the deed from a positive to a negative experience. Empress is finding her way into your life, in roles that are revered, perhaps a reversed or upside down. It could also mean that you are relying too much on others to make all of your decisions for you and to take care of you. You need to work towards building confidence in your own actions and reactions and removing this overbearing influence on your life. It is important that you always try your best to solve your problems on your own.

The Fool Tarot Card Description

We have covered the Fool tarot card throughout the book but this is a deeper look into the card. The Fool shows up as a young person walking happily in the world. He is enthusiastic, joyful, animated as he is taking his first steps. He does not care for the possible dangers of the world that lie in his path and carries nothing with him except a small sack of possessions. If he takes just a step more, he will likely fall off the cliff. He is so close to the edge and is soon to encounter the first of these possible dangerous situations. But this doesn't seem to concern the Fool. This means that we are not sure whether he is simply unaware or very naive. The dog nipping at his heels can be seen as a sign that if he does not turn out to be more aware of his surroundings and place in the world soon, he may never see all the adventures that he dreams of encountering come to completion, as the dog is an animal that barks at him in caution.

To see The Fool presented in a tarot spread in an upright position usually means a beginning of a new journey, one where you will be filled with a sense of freedom from the usual limitations in life and some level of optimism. He approaches each day as a new adventure, in what can be considered a childish way when we meet him. He believes that there are many opportunities that are lying out there in the world for us that are just waiting to be explored and developed and anything and everything can happen in life. The Fool leads a very simple life yet fulfilling life, does not seem troubled by not knowing all of the dangers that are possible for him to encounter ahead and having no worries.

When you pull a reversed Fool in your reading, you can usually find his more unconstructive individuality is being put on exhibit. It can mean that you are actually acting like a fool by disregarding the penalty of your bad ruling and actions. Like the young boy represented in the card, you don't see how dangerous of a location you have gotten physically into. A reversed Fool card can show that you are living in the instant and are not putting an effort to plan for the future. The reversed Fool meaning serves as a caution that you need to pay more attention to what is going around you so that people are not likely to take advantage of you. This card is here to alert you on something that may likely be too good to be accurate, like the dog that is shown in many versions of this card.

The Judgment Tarot Card Description

This card symbolizes what one would imagine the last ruling on earth would be, in the various forms many mythologies believe it will occur. The image in the Judgment card shows women, men, and children who are increasing from the grave to respond to Gabriel's call of his trumpet. Their outreached arms represent that they are ready to be judged by the gods as well as the universe. They are about to get together with their creator, their actions are to be looked at closely, and they are going to find out where they will spend the remainder of eternity. Could it possibly be Heaven or Hell? Remember that judgment is inescapable, the huge ocean wave in the background shows that this judgment will be final.

To see this card in an upright position, traditional Judgment meanings focus on the immediate when we reflect and appraise ourselves and our proceedings It is through self-likeness that we can have a sharper and more purpose about where we are now and what we need to do in order to continue to grow as humans. The

Judgment card appearing in a reading signifies that you are pending close to this significant point in your existence where you must start to assess yourself.

To see this card in a reverse or upside down position, this can mean that you doubt yourself and you are prone to judging yourself too cruelly. You are probably missing out on different life opportunities that are available to you because you do not see them. The lost drive makes it much more difficult to continue to move forward as you are falling behind in your plans. You should be moving forward with confidence and pride in yourself, and this means that you should not continue to be cautious.

The Star Tarot Card Description

The Star card shows us a woman who is kneeling at the rim of what looks like a small dew pond. She is holding what appears to be two water containers. One container pours the water out onto the land that appears to be dry, as if she is trying to nourish it and ensure it continues to be fertile. It seems to be working as there is lush green land all around her. In the water, she has one of her feet and this foot shows the spiritual ability and the inner power of the woman. The other foot located on the ground and shows her sense of strength and practical abilities. Behind her in the picture, there is a large middle star bounded by seven small stars which are chakras representations of the person. There is a bird appearing to be standing on a tree branch which is a symbol of the place are minds go to in thought. The Star's astrological sign is Aquarius.

To see The Star card in an upright position, your reading means that you have passed through and gone through what someone can consider an awful challenge in life. You have not lost a sense of hope as you have managed to get through this. Perhaps, you are not aware of your own strength while you know you have suffered, and that can get you through these situations, but you are now perhaps recognizing that the loss, although painful, helped you discover your own toughness and inner power. You can appreciate all that you are and all that you have become at this moment.

If you see the Star card reversed, it means that you are feeling as though the whole thing and everybody has turned in opposition to you. The challenges in life that you would usually see as thrilling seem instead to make you feel as though you cannot conquer them at all. You have lost confidence in something, whether inside yourself or with something you usually find beloved to you in your life.

The Temperance Tarot Card Description

On the Temperance card, there is what appears to be an angel with wings, whose gender is not immediately obvious as if it is male or female, which suggests that there is a balance between both of the sexes. One foot of the angel is in the water, to represent the subconscious mind, while the other foot is on dry land, which is a representation of the material world as we know it. On the robe, there is a square, which has a triangle inscribed inside. This can be another symbolization of the tangible earth in union with what we know as the holy trinity. The angel holds two cups in a manner where it can mix the waters together, which represents the conscious and subconscious minds. The water flows between them fluidly, suggesting a state of the union and infinity.

An upright Temperance in a spread may indicate a time to appraise and reexamine the priorities you have chosen for yourself in your life. This will help you create a balance between what is your outer and inner self. At the end of all the deeper investigation, you will find greater purpose and meaning in your actions, for the angel's message is that we cannot live fully in either one, we must have a balance between the two.

If the Temperance is reversed, it is a reflection of something that is out of balance and may be causing us stress and anxiety in our everyday lives. The real meaning of the Temperance card can be deciphered using the other cards in the spread to recognize areas where this imbalance could be caused. Temperance in reversal may also be used as a warning. This warning could be if you take a certain path, it would lead to turmoil and overload.

The Justice Tarot Card Description

The Justice tarot card is a symbol of law, fairness, and truth. The scales in her left hand represent how instinct should be the equilibrium of logic as she sits in the chair. She symbolizes impartiality with the double-edged sword that is located in her right hand. The lucidity in thought which is required to deal out justice is symbolized by the square on the crown she wears. Beneath her red cloak, which is held together by a clasp, she shows the tip of a white shoe. Behind her in the picture, there is a purple cloak and two standing grey pillars.

If you see the Justice card in a standing position, if you have been mistreated, this card's appearance may bring you liberation. In opposition to that, if your actions caused pain to other people, this card serves as a caution for those actions. Her manifestation represents a possibility for you to alter your proceedings now for a better prospect for yourself and others. When a figure of justice is shown on the tarot, it is time to own up to your actions.

A reversed Justice Tarot card in a spread could point to multiple outcomes. One Justice reversed meaning is to demonstrate to you that you are living in a condition of refutation. You are showing in reference to your actions and the actions of others you are unwilling to see the consequences. You have guilt and you are running away from it. These actions are in your past and you must be made aware. Your future depends only on your actions that are taken today and what you are willing to do in order to tip the scales back in equilibrium again. Give yourself you a chance to change your mind and stop judging yourself by taking action. This could represent an unfair result of a case that you will not be willing to accept in legal matters.

CHAPTER 6
Exploring Spreads

A tarot card spread is a predetermined and understood prototype for laying out the tarot cards that are pulled for a reading. The spread will determine how many cards will be pulled, where each one goes, and what each one will mean when it is revealed. A spread should be considered a template for showing the placement of the tarot cards so they can give more meaning to the topic at hand, depending on what the seeker wants to know. The meanings of the cards will come together to create a beautiful answer to the question within the template.

One of the most important features on the spread is that face that each individual place has its own sole connotation that brings light to the understanding of whatever card that is put in that spot when it is pulled. For instance, the Four of Pentacles stands for control, an inability to change, and possessiveness. Say this card was to be pulled and fall into the 4th Position of the Celtic Cross Spread, which is considered a position of the past, you would look at how the character of this card is beginning to move out and away from you. If it were to fall into the 6th position, which is for the future, you would instead see these characteristics as now coming into your present life. As you can see, this is a different interpretation just solely depending on where it lands in the pulls of the spread.

Tarot spreads vary in size and often pattern. One example is Rahdue's Wheel, which includes all 78 cards and creates a very enormous picture of a person's life. One card by itself can also be considered a spread. One card spreads are typically very useful in daily readings, if you chose to go this route in your tarot reading journey. The majority of spreads, however, contain between six and fifteen cards. This range is small enough to be managed by one person, especially if you are new to the practice, but it is also large enough to get deep enough into the answer of the question you are looking for. The pattern of the spread, the way in which the cards are pulled and placed, often forms a particular plan that reflects on the topic of the pull and spread. An example of this would be the

Horoscope Spread. In this shape of traditional circles, the cards will form what is known as a person's chart of birth. There are 12 cards in this spread, and the 12 cards represent the 12 houses of what is known to be astrology.

When cards are recognized to be connected in a spread, a completely fresh height of sense can be shaped. Combinations come into view and a more in-depth storyline is beginning to develop. It can include people, stories, and ideas about life. The creation of a story from the cards that are pulled in a spread is the most thrilling and absolutely the most imaginative aspect of the art of tarot reading. It is an art for sure, but there are still lots of guidelines that need to be followed.

You might be wondering what the most commonly used tarot spreads are. In no particular order, we will now discuss what are to be the most ordinary tarot spreads and how they can be used in your tarot reading practice.

The True Love Spread

It really is no shock that this is one of the most widely used spreads across all of tarot. Everyone would like to know where their true love is. Most people would like to know who their true love is, what is likely to happen in the romantic relationship they are currently in or hope to be in, and if they will be happy with the partner of their choosing. This spread is known to be very useful to evaluate relations with your spouse such as the emotional, spiritual, mental, and physical.

Six cards are in this spread. Card number one is you. It shows your current feeling about your relationship, your outlook, and your approach towards the relationship. Card two represents the partner. It will also represent the emotions they have towards you, expectations, and attitudes towards your relationship. Card number three is known as a card of connection. What are the characteristics that you both have that are keeping you together? Card number four indicates the power of your association. What are the characteristics of your relationship possesses that is keeping it together? Card number five is the representation of the weaknesses in your relationship. What are the things you need to improve upon in your relationship? Finally, card six is your true love card. This interprets what needs to be looked at and potentially changed in your relationship. Is your relationship likely to be long lasting? What can be done if there is a potential threat of failure?

The Success Spread

The Success Spread is an outstanding situational spread for use when you are up against a challenge or obstacle and do not know how to go about it. The spread is designed to help you better appreciate the true character of the challenge you face, as well as it being able to help you recognize what skills and other capital you have obtainable to help you face and conquer these obstacles.

This is a five card spread. The first card represents your major concern or challenge. The second card represents your current challenges and complications that you are wanting to know more about. Card number three is a revelation of the hidden factors you may not know, but in your current situation, you likely have a need to know. Card number four reveals fresh ideas, things, or people that can help you grow further in your life. Card number five is the indicator of what you should be doing so that you are successful and or what you should do in life to avoid ultimate failure.

The Celtic Cross Spread

Although it may look complex, the Celtic Cross spread has been used time and time again over the years. It is in its complexity that this spread also reveals its charm. This spread is most helpful in situations that are complicated, because it can be versatile and its positions give you a wide variety of information that can be read in lots of different ways that are all dependent on the combination of cards. It shows the issues at hand because of the seeker's actions, but it also shows that other people can be an influence that is contributing to the situation.

This is a 10 card spread. Card number one presents your current situation. Card number two is laid across card number one to tell you either what is doing positive things for you or what is keeping you from doing things. Card number three is all of your subconscious influences. Are you unaware of what your heart truly desires? These influences you are not aware of affect your everyday life. Card number four is your past card. Are there past instances and events that are influencing your life in a negative way now? A bad card in the past may be something you should get rid of as it is having a negative connotation to your current situation, and a good card in the past position should be an inspiration. Card number five represents your desires that you are aware of. Are there ideas or goals that are considered highly valuable to you in this current state? This is the area you should place all of your highest energy on. Depending on what card is pulled, it may also tell you how you put that energy to use. Card number six is your headlight. What path are you taking and where are you going? If there is a negative energy card pulled here, what are ways that you can avoid it? What ways can you reroute your path to get your life back on track? Card number seven is your current approach. It represents your ideals, thoughts, and actions. Card number eight is an energy card. What kind of energy do you get from the people who surround your life and your environment? Are they helpful or hurtful? Card number nine is a revelation card. It is a symbol of the things you should be aware of and bring consciousness to in your current situation. You should not disregard this card if it is shown. Card number 10 is the last card and it results in your final outcome. Based on your how your energies are currently being pulled, this will have a strong connection to your number five card. Are the energies in these cards conflicting or are they complementing one another?

The Spiritual Guidance Spread

This spread is very similar to the Success Spread. The Spiritual Guidance Spread is used during periods that you are feeling challenged or facing obstacles of religious life, usually relating to your own personal development and expansion. This type of spread is used to give you a wider viewpoint and includes information to guide you through your saintly expedition and imperative life education.

This is an 8-card spread. Card number one is your primary issue, question, or concern. Card number two interprets the motivation behind your quest for guidance. Card number three is an identifier of places during your life you are feeling disheartened or anxious. Card number four shows the proceedings that you are unaware of in your current situation. Card number five is your card of advice. It will give you the knowledge for actions that you should or should not take to conquer your doubts and anxiety. Card number six will tell you the way to move forward from your worries and what you will need to do in order to keep moving in the best way. Card number seven tells you how to continue to move forward in a positive way. Card number eight wraps up all of the different types of outcomes that you are likely to see if you use the tarot card as a guide to the light.

The Career Path Spread

If you are currently employed and feel like you have been stagnant in your position for a long time, or trapped in an occupation pothole for many years, wanting to be moved up but have been looked over, this is the spread for you. This spread is great for bringing awareness to any impediment you may have been seeing in your proficient life, and it will suggest strategies for you to deal with the issue at hand. This spread will also suggest alternative career paths based on your personal strengths if you are miserable in your current location.

This is a seven card spread. The first card interprets the answer to the question you may ask of your present job being your perfect job. The second card will symbolize actions that must be taken in order to keep your career moving forward. The third card will reveal things about your career life that you are not able to update or change. The fourth card shows your height of optimistic presentation in your present position. Are you putting forth the effort needed to get yourself to the next place or even begin advancing upward? The fifth card tells you the things that you need to look into changing and improving. The sixth card should answer the question: Is there an event in the past that is affecting your current work status? The seventh card is the one that tells you the result you should be looking for if you are to use the cards as a guide to how to change things.

The Three Card Spread

This is one of the simplest commonly used spreads. It is simply a pull of three cards. However, just because it seems simple, don't let that mislead you. This is one of the most influential tarot card spreads. This spread is one of the fastest ways to get guided to the answers to any questions you may have, and it can also provide you with leadership and imminent if you simply are feeling puzzled or misplaced. This is one of the most vibrant spreads by far, and it is effective at bringing forth the energies you are experiencing from the past, the present, as well as the future ones you will feel. The three card spread is not like the other spreads previously discussed. The 3-Card spread is different in the sense that there is not only one purpose for the spread or meaning for each of the cards. In its place, they can be completely vibrant and diverse depending on the point of the reading and the questions that are being asked. Below is a list of how the 3 card spread can be used.

1. What aids you / what stops you / what do you have the potential for?
2. Past/present/future
3. What you believe/ what you sense/what you carry out
4. Current situation/challenges/guidance
5. Strengths/weaknesses/advise
6. You/your partner/your relationship
7. Mind/body/spirit

These are just some of the most commonly used spreads to help get you started in your tarot card journey. Feel free to explore all of the other examples that will be discussed in the next chapter as we will begin to learn how to interpret your spreads based on the cards that you pull. As with everything in tarot, it will take practice but it will be to your advantage to take the time to learn these things early in your tarot journey so that you only progress and get better as your journey continues.

CHAPTER 7
Interpreting Your Spread

It is likely when you begin your tarot card reading journey that you will begin and pull a spread and realize you have no idea what the cards are actually trying to tell you! This is where you should understand it is important to seek help and understanding to learn how to interpret the cards you pulled in your spread. You may even be further along in your tarot reading journey and know what the book meanings of the cards are, but if you look at the spread in front of you, it might be hard to understand how the cards relate to you personally. You should know that each card can have several different meanings, but you may not know what meaning pertains to the question you asked. Everyone will have moments of doubting your ability or feeling overwhelmed, but the key is to find the right strategy that worked for you and stick with it throughout your journey.

Get your mind into a receptive mode

It should be stressed that this is an extremely important aspect of interpreting your tarot card spread. You may be asking what a receptive mode is. Think of it this way, a quiet mind is a receptive mind. You will be able to notice more images and be more receptive to the messages for the spirits if and when you are in the right frame of mind to receive them. Some believe that doing their readings in the morning helps them become more receptive because your mind is generally quieter before the day really begins. This will help you already be in a receptive mode if you are not already going through the motions of your day to day life.

Whether you do your readings in the morning, afternoon, or evening it is important to take the time to center yourself and get into your receptive mind before you begin pulling your spread. If your mind is all over the place, how can you expect to receive any messages from your own higher self or from spirit? This can be like walking up 20 flights of stairs when there is an elevator right by it!

Work smarter not harder also pertains to tarot card readings. Here is an example guide on how to get you into a receptive mode:

1. Begin by taking a few deep and steady breaths, imagine a white and soft light beginning to fill your body.
2. Hold your breath for a few moments and feel the light begin to relax your body and cleanse all of your cells.
3. Exhale. As you do so, breathe out all your thoughts and troubles of your mind. Let everything go for the moment.
4. Repeat these steps as many times as you feel necessary to get yourself ready to receive the message.

That's it! It really is that easy! You can use any type of visualization you want. If you are not a visualization type person, you can also listen to uplifting music or anything that helps you obtain a calm mind and body.

Asking the right question will get you the right answer

Asking the right question is key to getting the answers you are looking for in a spread. A vague question will render you an equally vague response. The cards will pick up exactly what you are asking as you shuffle the cards in the deck. Sometimes you may ask a certain type of question, but you really mean something else than what you are asking. Then it is likely you will look at the cards you pulled and be confused because it does not seem to relate. If the question you are asking does not make sense, you cannot expect your answer to make any sense either. It is important for you to be crystal clear about what you are really asking.

Tarot cards will answer the question you are asking in a long form, never in short form. The responses you get are not going to be a straight forward yes or no, they will likely be telling you a story. So, this should help you to understand you should avoid asking yes and no questions. The pendulum is the perfect instrument for yes or no questions and probabilities. The tarot gives you a detailed explanation.

What can you do instead of asking yes or no questions? You should be asking open-ended questions for more long-form responses. For example, instead of asking the tarot if you will get the job you are interviewing for, you should ask what you can do to get the job instead. Remember to break down your questions into different sections in order to get a clearer picture of the situation. From here, you can divide and conquer. Begin your questions with what, why, and how.

You have a gut, trust it!

The first impression you get from your tarot spread is usually the right one. Remember this, write it down, and frame it if you have to! This is the most important thing to remember when it comes to intuitive tarot card reading. You can deal out three cards and your heart tells you one thing, but it doesn't necessarily match the book meaning. So which meaning is the one you should go with? Always go with the meaning you are initially drawn to first whether or not it is what the books say! The book meanings are there to help us when we are at a learning state, to get a feel for the cards using them for the first time, and to be familiar with how a reading situation should feel. You will have to rely on intuition to know which meaning to apply in which situation. You should use the book meanings as a basis to get you started but what really moves the reading forward into outer space is your intuition!

What should you do if you get stuck in a reading?

1. Pay attention to your feelings. What sensations or emotions do you feel when you look at the cards?
2. Pay close attention to any words, images, or thoughts that enter your mind when you look at the cards.
3. Look for any repeating symbols or things within the images that capture your eye first.

Let your intuition point the way! It will never lead you to the wrong place. Whatever your gut feeling is, you should just go with it as you continue to practice.

Throw your assumptions out of the window

You need to throw your preconceived assumptions out the window when practicing tarot reading. Sometimes if we are in a difficult situation, we make assumptions about what the outcome will be and about what the other person or people in the situation are thinking or feeling. We may ask the cards the question, but we think we already have the answer in our mind. Note, however, this is not the same thing as trusting your gut, which we just discussed. This is when you assume things based on your own fear and insecurities. Tarot will tell you what you need to know, not what you want to know.

An example, you have been having some difficulties with a friend and you are thinking to yourself "she does not want to hang out with me anymore because she thinks that she is better than me" or something similar. You deal out the cards and you are feeling stumped by what you pulled because you may be looking at them but you are not actually seeing them. You are not letting the cards do the talking like they should. You do not see the forest for the trees! Sometimes three cards that make no sense to you before will make absolute sense to you after the face. This is because you will realize afterward that you were making assumptions that were blocking you from truly understanding the meaning of the cards at the time you pulled them. It could have actually been that your friend was truly busy and was not able to hang out and that is the reason why you got the card that you did. What you can do instead is just try to put your assumptions aside that you may have already made and look at the cards and nothing else. Let them tell you the story they are trying to tell.

Keep an eye out for dominance

One last thing that can help you understand the messages coming through to you from the cards is to take a step back and look at the spread on an overall level. What you want to do here is to look for the dominant suits or absences of the major arcana cards, individual suits, court cards, or numbers. This will tell you what the situation is about through the dominances and what energy is not present at the time through the absences.

For example, let us say that you drew cards for a spread and half of them were majors. A dominance of majors in the spread means that the issue is something that is important to you for your path in life: a life lesson, part of your destiny, or karmic reasons behind it. These things are not easy to change. It means that there are larger forces that are working here. The opposite is true if no majors are pulled at all. A lot of court cards pulled in a spread are a clue that this is a situation where many people are involved and there could be a potential clashing of personalities. It could be that you are in a situation and the people around you all have different individual options about the situation.

As stated, dominances and absences tell you what type of energy is surrounding the reading you are doing and what it is about. Wands indicate that the situation is one centered with passion, establishing, and creativity. A lot of cups means the main thing that is of concern are emotions, relationships, intuition, and how people feel about things. A lot of swords mean that the situation is centered on mental energy, communication, and interpersonal conflict or aggression. A lot of pentacles mean that the issue is mainly about health, education, money, or other material concerns. Pentacles are a practical suit. For example, say you want to know what to do in a particular situation. You pull three cards and all are minor arcana, 2 of the 3 cards are from the same suit. Just by looking at the dominances, you can see that the advice that is coming across is to consider the emotions of all of the people involved or if you are asking about something that does not involve others, then you should be trusting your gut and going with your intuitions.

Find the connections between the images

The images in the cards are the first thing to tell you a story. Think of them like living images that all interact with one another. Begin by just taking a look at the pictures and see the overall scene. Notice what it looks like and what it could mean about the question you are asking. Some things to look for:

- Do certain figures in the scene appear to be facing each other as if in agreement, or are they facing away from each other in disagreement?
- Do the figures in the cards look like they are pointed to the other ones in the spread or are they looking in the direction of another card?
- Are the cards looking forward to the future or looking back towards the past?
- Do the cards look like they are a part of the same scene or a different part of a scene in the same place? For example, two cards have a set of mountains in the background. Could it be the same set of mountains just from different perspectives?

It will force you to think outside the box and add a layer of your own interpretations on top of the book when you look at the cards this way. When you start thinking of the cards differently, you can really begin the journey of unlocking your abilities as an intuitive card reader. The key point to take away from this section is that the book meanings of the cards are just a starting point of reference in the beginning of your tarot journey. It is ultimately up to you to decide the meaning you want to go with, according to your own intuition and your internal feelings.

CHAPTER 8
Practice Examples

Tarot case studies are perfect for resources for anyone who wanted to teach themselves how to read tarot cards. These examples may also be valuable to anyone who enjoys receiving tarot readings and wants to get more insight as to how they can apply the tarot reading to their life outside of the reading. We will divide the tarot card reading examples into four categories, and we will cover a different example for the topics. The categories we will cover are love, career, wellbeing, and social.

Love and Relationship Examples

The subjects in the first case study are both divorced with children who are older adults. They would like to make a relationship worth together and maybe even eventually move in together. The problem they are facing seems to be that they are losing the magic feeling they felt when they first got together. In this example, you will want to do a five card pull. The card meanings will be as follows: His baggage, her baggage, moving forward, his growth, and finally, her growth.

Which of his issues have been affecting our relationship the most?

Say in this instance, a Queen of Swords card is pulled for the first position. Choosing the Queen of Swords suggests that your partner has likely experiences an injustice at one point or another. This may have been acted against him, or he was the one who was acting unfairly. It may also represent him behaving unjustly to himself, as in that he can constantly put others' rights above his own. This is a time for the truth and honesty to help your partner see more clearly and move forward to integrity. He will therefore need to find the balance by adopting the spirit of the Queen of Swords

What issues am I bringing to the relationship?

Say that the Ten of Wands is pulled for the second position. The Ten of Wands in this position suggest you may have been feeling a sense of being weighed down previously. It is likely you have been taking on too much or taking responsibility for other people's problems unnecessarily. These burdens you have been carrying may now be having a negative effect on you. Ask yourself if you are or have been feeling stressed and burnt-out. This may be your body giving you the message to slow down.

What is the best thing to do to help our relationship?

Say that the Empress is pulled for this third card position. If you want to bring more peace to yourself and to the ones that are around you, act as the empress does, with understanding and compassion. If you find yourself in a situation where you feel frustrated by those people who are around you, just remember you do not need to change anyone. Just learn to love them as they are and watch them change before your eyes. This love can and usually needs to especially apply to yourself. Learn how to treat yourself with compassion and you too can be transformed.

How will this relationship help him grow?

Say that the Ace of Swords was pulled for this fourth card position. The Ace of Swords in this fourth position suggests your boyfriend or significant other will face an empowering challenge once you have worked on the relationship and made it better. Tackling this problem will allow him to really grow as a person and as a partner. The situation may be an ongoing one that he has already been experiencing or it may be a new test for him. Either way, he will benefit from seeing the 'problem' as an opportunity for him to grow. It is an opportunity for him to gain strength and demonstrate courage, knowing it may require him to locate great inner resources. Your boyfriend may find that his understanding of problems will change as a result of this change in his current attitude, and thus his approach to life's battles will become much healthier and more rewarding.

How will the relationship help me grow?

Say that the Tower card was pulled for this fifth and final position. The pulling of the Tower and its presence in the tarot card pull suggests you will face authoritative and encouraging changes once you have resolved your personal issues. Before this happens, you may be able to feel an inactive feeling in the air like the kind you feel just before a strong thunderstorm breaks open the sky and begins to rain. If the storm does break, then welcome it with open arms. If not, see what you can do to make big changes yourself on your own terms. You should not expect an easy ride when the Tower card appears, but keep in mind how much more peaceful the world seems after a strong storm.

The next example is a reading taken by a couple who are in the mid-thirties and they were married very young. At this time, they are going through a bit of a rough patch in their relationship. He is having difficulties committing to a job and she feels like she is not being supported as she is bringing up all three of their children. His sense of limbo and her struggles are brought out in the cards. In this example, you will want to pull six cards. The card meanings are as follows: the husband, the wife, his potential, her potential, his guidance, and her guidance respectively.

What is the husband experiencing in the marriage?

Say that the Hanged Man is pulled for the very first card position. This card suggests the husband may be hanging in limbo at this time. This corresponds directly with the idea that he cannot commit to a job. He could be feeling that his situation has reached an impasse. If he wants things to move on for his career, he needs to try a different approach towards sticking with a job. Is there a more creative way for him to find a way to move forward? The husband may find that the key to unlocking his dilemma is to work out what it is he needs to give up or what sacrifices he could make at this time. This could mean letting go of a part of himself which is getting in his way without him even realizing it. His surrender will likely move him forward where other ways have failed in similar situations.

What is the wife experiencing in the marriage?

Say that the Five of Coins is pulled for this second position in the spread. This card suggests the wife is going through a difficult situation at this time. She may have very little energy or motivation to focus on what is in front of her or she may feel she is just 'getting by' in day in and day out experiences. Perhaps she is only motivated to deal with the basic necessities of life and not anything above and beyond that. Or perhaps she is not even able to do that, which is also a likely possibility. This may be a time, however, when a new spiritual awareness becomes known inside her, as the other, more temporary aspects of her life fall by the wayside.

How will the husband grow in the marriage?

Say that the Queen of Cups is pulled in this 3rd position of the spread. Pulling the Queen of Cups in this position suggests the husband will find himself in an environment of absolute love in his married life. This may be exactly what he needs to see and feel if things have been difficult for him recently. The card also suggests that someone may require the husband's love, such as his wife and children. He should try not to question or resist this love when it comes or if and when he is asked to show it, but just accept that this is what is needed for him and of him. The card asks that when the husband receives love, he should remember to give in return as much as he can, as he is being asked to generally work towards a more loving and caring world.

How will the wife grow in the marriage?

Say that the Seven of Wands is pulled in the 4th position. Pulling the Seven of Wands in this position predicts the wife will find a sense of great courage within herself in her married life. This inner strength will most likely carry her over whatever hurdles she needs to face and will see her through all kinds of troubles she may previously have felt was impossible to tackle on her own. All areas of the wife's life will improve when she can access this important power inside her.

What is the best thing the husband can do to support his marriage?

Say that the Hermit was pulled for this 5th position. This is a suggestion you need time by yourself if the Hermit is present now. As in this is a period of seeing your inner self where exterior distractions are restricted. This card reminds us of that part of ourselves deep within that is always searching for a deeper understanding and the card asks us to get rid of that need through being alone and consideration. You are losing touch with your soul and inner self as there is a potential for a lot of different things to be going on in your life right now. It is likely you are going to external factors to research and find answers to the problems that you have. However, the Hermit tells you that within yourself, you will find the answers and if you are looking to others to solve your problems, it is possible for you to forget who you are as a person. Therefore, if you take this time to reflect and be alone, you should be able to get back to your old self. There should be a feeling of being fulfilled and peacefulness if you are able to do this.

What is the best thing the wife can do to support her marriage?

Say that the Ace of Wands was pulled for the sixth and final position. The appearance of the Ace of Wands in this position once it is pulled for this position advises you to notice any seeds of creative ideas or daydreams you might be having and plant them in the fertile ground as soon as possible. Now is an excellent time for forming new plans, making some important decisions, realizing your dreams, and manifesting your visions, so care for the growth of these creative seeds and defend them until they flower. Following through on your visions could become transformative for you and it can also bring tremendous adventure and vibrancy to your life. In the future, you will find yourself more in a casual flow of life and feel it is far easier to be naturally inventive. If you are feeling a sense of being stuck at this time, you should apply lateral thinking to your situation in order to move through obstacles and hindrances.

Work and Money Example

In this example, the seeker is a mother of two children who are school age. She works very long and tiring hours in human resources and she does not get to see her kids as much as she would like. She is starting to see her job is taking a toll on her family and on her health. She wants to know if she should pull back on her hours and spend more of her time resting and being a mom. In this example, you will want to pull five cards. The card meanings in their positions are as follows: work, life, prioritize work, prioritize life, balancing.

How are things going for me at work?

Say that the Strength card is pulled in the first position of this spread. The appearance of the card pulled in this position indicates that you may be lacking a sense of inner strength currently. This strength may be what is necessary to help you deal with a variety of difficult situations, but instead perhaps you are unable to manage and cope and are therefore leaving things undone, or are not doing them in the most satisfactory and complete way. You may honestly be on the verge of giving up. It is important to remember that the qualities of courage and strength are always available to you, but you will need to believe in yourself as well as your inner power in order to access them.

How are things going in my non-work life?

Say that the Knight of Wands is pulled for the second position in this spread. Pulling the Knight of Wands is an indication that you may be behaving irresponsibly or acting recklessly at the moment. This may have negative repercussions for you or possibly to others around you. For instance, is it possible you are acting insensitively towards someone? Or is it possible that you are excessively going out late at night, drinking heavily, gambling or spending in excess of what you can afford? Even if you are not behaving this terribly, the card still shows you what elements of your life in some way have become out of balance and you can see that it is causing some problems. There may be some fundamental anxieties or pressures that could result in a sense of being unbalanced, and your behavior might be more indicative of this but it is not a reflection of what you are like as a person. If so, you should try to find out the causes of this bad behavior and ask yourself how you can figure out how to stop them in order that you can return to your normal self again in a positive way.

What would happen if I decided to prioritize work?

Say that the Three of Wands was pulled for this third position. Receiving the Three of Wands in this card pull says that you are very likely to put yourself into new horizons if you spend more time at work. You will live more adventurously, be able to accomplish many of your goals, and will also review wisely the hurdles in front of you, making smart, educated choices as to how to attempt them. Seeing these obstacles as challenges will allow you to achieve a healthy approach to life's ups and downs. You should then be able to achieve great things.

What would happen if I prioritized other parts of my life?

Say that the Devil card is pulled in this 4th position. Pulling the devil card in this position suggests you may often be tempted if you spend more time away from work. This temptation could be from outside forces or inside yourself or a mixture of the two and could cause you problems if you follow through with it. However, it is certain that the means for meeting this attraction will be found within you. If you can look impartially at your own 'inner devil' or saboteur and find the strength to combat him, you will not only find yourself back on the straight and narrow path in your life, but will also feel a sense of accomplishment, pleasure, and decency as a result. Remember, temptations can be there to test us, and tests we pass will ultimately be rewarded.

How can I get guidance to integrate work better into my life?

Say that the Star is pulled for this fifth and final position. The Star in this position recommends you to look around or inside you for control in your life. Maybe there is someone in your life who can help to keep you on track at this time. But perhaps the guiding star will come from within your own self. The Star is a good sign that your future is looking good but you need to preserve an optimistic approach towards this future in order to get you through any difficult patches.

Family and Friends Example

In this example, the seeker in this reading is trying to persuade her sister to move out of the city she has lived in for the last twenty years and move closer to her family and her mother. She is stubborn and resistant to change. Even though she no longer has a career or anything for her in the city, she makes excuses as to why she cannot move. This is a four card spread. The meanings of the positions of the cards are as follows: Her past, her life, advice, and her future.

What has happened to my sister to make her act the way she does?

Say that the Nine of Coins is pulled in this very first position. Pulling the Nine of Coins card right now is an indication your sister may have been unable to feel happiness in her life before. Perhaps she has been too hard on herself with work or maybe she has simply turned her attraction off of the good that is happening in her. It is possible that she feels that she does not deserve these things that she does have, or is it possible that she has been feeling symptoms of depression? She might also have noticed herself feeling more tired than usual, as she may have been lacking her usual energetic self. This card could tell your sister to open her consciousness to what she has been blessed with and be thankful for the things that she has that makes her happy, or to buy herself something she would enjoy, in order to remind her that she deserves that level of happiness.

What are the important issues my sister is facing?

Say that the Seven of Coins is pulled for this second position. This card suggests that your sister is feeling she has reached an area of stability at this time. Perhaps she senses that the life journey she has been on for quite some time is becoming less important to her life as new people are coming into her life and it is likely that her situations are not what they once were. She could also be feeling that she has less eagerness for pursuing what she wants in her life. These feelings often point to that a time of expression and meditation is necessary. This may be a time for your sister to echo upon her plans and perhaps alter them in order to put her on a path that holds more meaning in her future.

Is there anything I can do to help my sister?

Say that the Eight of Cups is pulled for this 3rd position. The Eight of Cups in this position shows you to pay attention to where you feel aggravated or fidgety. The card is telling you to pay attention to feelings, as they might be trying to tell you where you have a lack of accomplishment, or where it may be the right time in your life to start on other things. Notice the things in life that gave you joy at one point but no longer mean anything to you. You should change these things or get rid of them. It might be a good time to search your soul in order to bring your conscious and subconscious more in line together and lead a life more along the lines of what you are supposed to be doing. This could be a time of both happiness and or sadness: you feel sad because you are giving up something you are aware of, and the happiness is seeing that there is a more bountiful path for you to take. Always be aware of the future and what it has the possibility of bringing to you. If prayer is your thing, you should look to a higher power and allow the higher power to guide you to a path that best matches what you are set out to do in life.

How will things develop in my sister's life?

Say that the Chariot card is pulled for this 4th and final position. The manifestation of The Chariot suggests your sister will likely have the chance to move on past the obstacles and difficulties she is facing in the future. She has the opportunity to face them head-on like a warrior princess or she can hide away from them in fear. The first one will require her to have the strength of mind and being accountable for herself and will be satisfied by an interlude of calm and self-reassurance, knowing that the battles of her life are now conquered. If your sister decides to shy away from them because she doesn't know how to handle the problem, she will be stripped of the possibility of putting the problems in her past and learning from them before she moves on. Therefore, she needs to put on a brave face and bring the Chariot spirit into her and push forward.

CHAPTER 9
Intuition Development For Insightful Readings

As you have come to realize through reading this book, there is more to tarot reading than just memorizing endless tarot card pictures and their meanings. It is also about knowledge to expand your own instinct and reassuring your mind so that your insight and perception have a chance to come through and grow. Intuition can be explained as your gut feeling. It is that intelligent part of yourself that is able to tap into imperceptible energies to make you aware of what you need to do at this point in your life.

Intuition and intellect are different. Intellect is your mind. Your mind should be good at seeing things that are going on in the physical world and finding out this information. Intuition is the senses and feelings of the surrounding energies and gives you this information in the form of feelings that are bodily, like gut feelings and hunches. The mind and your intuition act in harmony or they can always be in a sense of disconnect. For example, you may meet a new person who at first glance looks nice, has good manners, and is nice to everyone but you are feeling like you should not trust them and you do not like them almost right away. If you have an instant reaction to someone like this without having any physical evidence to back up the feeling, it can obviously be a bit uncomfortable. In your mind, you might begin to list all of the reasons why you think the person should be trustworthy, and that you should have no reason to disbelieve them. Yet, feel better when you are not around them.

Intuition is something that almost everyone is born with and as children, we are much more likely to trust it. However, through experiences that happen to us in life, we tend to disregard it more often than not and by the time we have grown as adults, it is likely we do not look to our intuition at all, we only use our mind. Now that we are used to this, the voice in our head that is our intuition gets quieter and impossible to hear. There are many things that block us from hearing our intuition as we get older.

- Over thinking/Active Minds
- Fear and worry
- Instances in culture tell us to disregard our initial feelings
- Judgments and assumptions
- Desires and expectations

By connecting with your body and breath and quieting your mind, you will allow your intuition to have a space of its own to allow for its voice to be heard again. Regular meditation is known to help people with this. Below are some steps you can follow to develop your intuition through meditation.

Step One
Find a space that is calm where you will not be troubled or broken up for a few minutes. This space is preferably a Zen enthused backyard with flora and fauna that are chirping happily and a stream that is babbling.

Step Two
Begin by sitting right up in a chair with your two feet flat on the floor surface and your hands resting on your lap. If it is comfortable for you, place your palms facing up. Sitting comfortably in a chair allows you to take your focus away from your body and its location and into your inner mind away from physical thoughts and feelings.

Step Three
Start to calm your mind. Your mind is not causing any problems, it is that it has to run all the time and it is hard for it to shut off at the blink of an eye. Say a quick thank you to your mind as it has done much for you over the years. Now you can ask it to be silent for a few minutes so that your intuition can begin to show through.

Step Four
You will want to set your intentions at the beginning of each session. Let your intuition know that you are showing up for it, you are ready to accept its message, and you will be judgment-free about what it has to say.

Step Five
Focus on how you are breathing for a few minutes. Do not try to change the level and pace of your breathing, just be mindful of it and pay attention to its repetition.

Step Six
Begin to pay attention to how you are feeling in your body. If you are not relaxed and you find yourself thinking about things as your mind is still wandering, try to use your breath in an exhale to remove the thought or feeling from your mind and body. You can even tell yourself to remove it with the exhales if that helps you in the beginning.

Step Seven
Be quiet as you sit for a little while and pay attention to the things that may be trying to come towards you. Pay attention to your physical feelings, insights, or ideas.

Once your meditation is complete, you may feel the urge to draw a card and look at it for a few minutes. Think about what you are feeling as you look at the card. If you find that your higher being and your intuition would want to send you a message through the card that you just pulled, what do you believe that message should be? Basically, the idea of learning how to get rid of all of the things that block you from your natural path to intuition is learning how you should develop your intuition. Learning to trust all the information that is given to you via your intuition from your inner energies is another way to develop your intuition.

CHAPTER 10
Reading For Others

Each reader of the tarot will have a different answer to the question of how to conduct a reading for others. Tarot readers are able to read the cards in many different ways. You learn a lot more by actually pulling the tarot cards so do not worry if you are not feeling very confident when you first start out. Over time, you will begin to understand each card more and more and then your card readings will become more in-depth and richer. Beginners can give very good readings right away just by trusting their intuition during the pull.

You probably are aware that you should review the basics before you try reading for someone else. You will want to know the different cards and their meanings before you do a reading. You will want to study the major arcana and all four of its suits so you can easily identify it on the spread. As a Reader, if you are more intuitive, you will likely get slightly different meanings from the custom manuscript taught representation but that is okay as we have learned. The point is, be aware of what you are doing before doing it for someone you know. If you only partially learn the meanings, you will only give a partial reading.

You will want to decide if you are comfortable using the reversal meanings in your reading. Lots of tarot readers read the card with the same meaning if it is upright or upside down. Others will follow the opposite meanings that can be applied to the card. It is your choice if you want to read the reversed card meanings, but it is a good idea to do the same thing each time you do a reading. In other words, if you want to do reverse meanings, do it in every reading you do, not just on the occasion that it works better. The cards will become very mixed as they are shuffled.

In some traditional Tarot readings, the reader will select a card to represent the Seeker, the person that is asking the question. This is sometimes referred to as a Signifier card. In some traditions, the signifier is selected based on maturity level and age. A king would be a good choice for an older man, while a page or a knight card would do well for a younger, less experienced male. You can also choose a card for personality. Your earthy sister may be represented by the Empress or your really devout brother is really well represented by the Hierophant. If you do not want to start assigning cards to the Seeker, you do not have to.

It is a good idea to have the Seeker shamble the deck so the cards can pick up on his or her energies. If you feel the Seeker has some negativity attached to him or her, you will want to cleanse the deck after the reading so that there is no residual negative energy that stays attached to your tarot card deck. If you really do not want the Seeker to shuffle, at the very least you should allow him or her to cut the deck into three piles after shuffling is done. As he or she does so, the Seeker should silently ask a simple but important question on which the reading will focus. Ask the Seeker to keep the question to them until the reading is done. Asking the question in their head while shuffling is the best way to do this.

You should then decide the type of layout you want to use. Some people prefer the Celtic Cross, others the Romany Method, or you can make up your own depending on the person you are reading. Start at the top of the deck, and place the cards in the order that the spread you choose says. As you turn the cards over, flip them from one side to the other, rather than vertically to be read. If you turn them vertically, a card that should be reversed will end up right side up and vice versa. Before you begin reading any of them, place all the cards in the layout in front of you all at once. Put the remaining cards in the deck aside when you are done pulling. This is when you can start to look over the cards before you read them.

Look over the spread, and look for any patterns or repeating symbols. For example, do you see more of one suit than another? Are there a lot of court cards, or no cards from the Major Arcana? Note the suits as well, because this will give you an idea of the way of the interpretation. Now that you have looked at the cards over methodically, it is time to do your interpretation. Trust in yourself and your instinct and you will have a very good reading for your Seeker!

Although it may be intimidating to give readings to other people, you will find that it will actually help you become more confident in your readings, the more you do them for others. You may find it easier to read for friends that you know because you do not have to prove anything to them.

If you get stuck during a reading, do not worry! It is possible it is a reflection of the person you are reading for, not your ability. They may be experiencing a sense of being stuck at some point in their life. Work through this feeling with them. The best way to overcome it is to talk about it with them. If you find that you just can't feel what the card is trying to tell you, go with the basic meaning of the card. So start by explaining the card to the person about what it is about, just like you might read in a tarot book. From here, you should be able to develop a more in-depth reason behind the card pull.

If you think that you need to stop yourself from sharing something from the spread because you do not want to offend that person, it is possible it will have a negative effect on your reading. It is your responsibility to say what is there, whether it is positive or negative. If you do not want to say negative things in a negative way, put a positive connotation on it. Tarot card reading is about understanding. It is for the person to develop a better understanding of the situation they are in and how they can use the advice from the reading to move forward and start fresh once they have figured out how to handle the problem.

CONCLUSION

Thank you for making it through to the end of *Tarot Reading Made Easy*! It is our sincere hope that this book was easy to follow and was very informative as you are beginning your journey through tarot card reading. Feel free to refer back to any one of these chapters when you feel necessary or pick it up often if you would like a quick read to reignite your passion for the craft and remembering some of the information you may have forgotten. This book is a really good reference for beginners who are getting started but it is also great for those who have been reading tarot cards for a while who just need a quick pick up and go reference guide!

The next step is to use what you have learned in this book and put it into practice with your tarot card reading. Remember that even if you forget a certain definition of a card or what the symbols on the card stand for, you can always refer back to this book and get a better understanding. You can also use this book to remember how to gain better intuition in your tarot card readings when you become more advanced in your practice. Take it step by step and remember what you learned in this book, and you will be reading for yourself and hopefully for others before you know it.

It is important to us that you look to your tarot card reading journey with an open heart and mind and we hope that this book has helped you feel more confident in getting started. Tarot is an interesting craft that has long been rooted in tradition and history and it is not only something for you to enjoy, but it is likely you can share it with others and they will truly come to enjoy it too. If you want to learn more about the history of tarot, there are many great resources online that will help you get a better understanding of where tarot came from and how it has adapted to the many cultures of the world as time and years have gone by.

Remember that there are many different types of spreads for different questions but you can always make up your own if you feel that it would better fit for an answer to a question that you are asking. You can always do daily readings on yourself to make sure you are keeping in check with your inner self and allowing your intuition to guide you through life more than your conscious mind. You may find that this approach to life will give you a broader view of the world and help you make better and more concrete decisions.

Finally, if you found this book useful in any way, a review on Amazon is always appreciated! Reviews help us to gain an understanding of what tarot card readers are looking for and how we can better understand what people need when they start out on their tarot card reading journey. If you feel that this book has helped you in any way, please also feel free to refer this book to your friends and family who are also looking into tarot and beginning their journey to reading the cards. Having a shared common ground will help you learn more about your friends and family and you can lean on each other for strength and guidance when you start reading a card or if you want to further develop your experience by reading for each other.

DESCRIPTION

Tarot Reading Made Easy is a helpful guide for beginners to learn all about tarot card reading and how to get started doing your own readings. The book will guide you through a brief history of what tarot is and where it came from, and how it has been shifted and changed throughout history and developed by different cultures to fit their needs. You will find that tarot cards are plenty and there are many different decks that have beautifully illustrated images to help you find the symbolism of each card. The book is structured to ease you through the art of tarot in this way:

- The book will begin with a brief history of the art of tarot and where it was first discovered and used and the history behind the first deck of tarot cards that are still in existence.

- You will then learn about what the major arcana is and the tarot cards in the deck that is associated with the major arcana. You will learn that these cards have different meanings than the rest of the cards in the deck.

- After you learn what the major arcana is and the cards that are in that part of the deck, you will learn the same things about the minor arcana. This part of the deck has its own cards and suits and they have their own unique meanings as well.

- The book will then cover the symbolism behind the illustrations on the cards and what each card is meant for and what it stands for. There will be an entire chapter on major arcana cards with a deep description of the cards and what you can do with them. This is an important section to refer back to as you continue through your journey.

- The book will then cover the different types of spreads you can use in your tarot card reading pulls and what each one stands for and when best to use them. It will also give you different spread pull examples so that you can see how to best interpret cards in the particular spread you choose.

- Finally, the book will wrap up with how to begin doing readings for other people. There is a quick guide on how to get started and simple tips to follow to make sure your readings for others are successful.

This book is a general guide to tarot reading and it is best for beginners or those who have been practicing tarot for a while and want to get a refresher course on things they likely already know but may have forgotten. If you have been interested in learning to read tarot cards for a while but did not know where to start, you have come to the right place! You will enjoy how easy this book is to read and the way that it guides you through the different topics that are related to tarot. This book will cover everything you need to know to get started reading tarot and the descriptions of the cards are general knowledge until you use the chapter on intuition building in order to make your own meanings for the cards when you look at them in the spreads. There is a flow to the book that will help even the newest person to tarot begin reading cards successfully once they finished this book.

www.ingramcontent.com/pod-product-compliance
Lightning Source LLC
Chambersburg PA
CBHW071506070526
44578CB00001B/456